DAILY BLESSINGS

FOR MY

Wife

Daily Blessings for My Wife
ISBN: 979-8-88898-139-9 - *Paperback*
ISBN: 979-8-88898-140-5 - *Hardcover*
ISBN: 979-8-88898-141-2 - *Ebook*

Cover Design by Faille Schmitz.
Manuscript written by Christopher Douglas.

He who finds a wife finds a good thing, and
obtains favor from the Lord.

PROVERBS 18:22 NKJV

My Dear Wife,

I have so much to tell you.

I know I'm not always the best at putting deeply felt things into words, but I want you to know how much I love you, how much you mean to me, and how important our marriage is.

I chose this little hook because it explains a lot of the things I think and feel when it comes to us and our relationship. I hope that as you read it, you will know that these letters and prayers reflect my heart and my love for you.

I long to see us grow closer. I want to get better at sharing my feelings and listening to yours. I want our friendship to get stronger and our love to become a rock-solid foundation supporting a marriage that will last and last.

Because I love you,

Your Husband

I'll Love You forever

My Dear Wife,

My love for you is endless. I know I don't always show it, and I admit that I sometimes get distracted with the demands of life and the pressures of work. But I want you to know that my love for you is here to stay—it's going to go the distance. I am committed to you, and I'm committed to our marriage. I plan to love you for all of my days.

I'm aware that things don't always go smoothly in our marriage and that we have our ups and downs, but through it all, one thing will never change—my love for you. I know it will go on and on. And I know that it will continue to increase and strengthen over time. My love for you is forever.

Dear God,

remind us that love is more than a feeling— it is a commitment to hang in there through thick and thin.

Help us as we daily choose to love like that—and enjoy what comes of it.

Amen.

You Were Made for Me

You made all the delicate, inner parts of
my body, and knit them together in my
mother's womb.

PSALM 139:13 TLB

My Dear Wife,

You are so perfect for me. Sometimes I can hardly believe how right you are for me. I'm not just talking about looks; although, you look great! I'm talking about things like your heart, your mind, your spirit. They all seem to complement my own. Yet at the same time, we are so completely different—almost opposites. I am so thankful that you're not like me. I am so glad you are you.

You complete me in many ways. You help me to act more thoughtfully instead of just letting me blunder along. You show me how to open up to my feelings. I can't even imagine what I'd be like without you in my life. And I don't ever want to find out. You were made for me—and I'm so thankful.

Dear God,

thank You for the way You have made us and brought us together. Remind us daily to celebrate our differences and the many ways we complement each other.

Amen.

I Promise You

For this reason a man shall leave his father
and mother and be joined to his wife, and
the two shall become one flesh.

EPHESIANS 5:31 NKJV

My Dear Wife,

I bless you for honoring our vows. I remember the day, my love, when we repeated our wedding vows. I was nervous, my palms were sweaty, and I longed for the whole thing to hurry up and end. But at the same time, I wanted it to go on forever. You were so beautiful, my bride. I still remember the sparkle in your eyes as you walked down the aisle toward me. On that day, I promised, before God and the whole world, to love and to cherish you for the rest of your days.

I still stand by that promise—maybe even more now than I did then, for now I better understand the significance of such a vow. Here and now, I promise you that I will be committed to our marriage for the rest of my life. I love you.

Dear God,

bless us as we reaffirm
our promise to love
and cherish each other
for all of our days.

Amen.

The First Time We Met

My darling, you are like a mare among the
king's stallions. Your cheeks are beautiful
with ornaments, and your neck with
jewels.

SONG OF SOLOMON 1:9-10 NCV

My Dear Wife,

Y ou are still my lovely one. I remember the first time I saw your face, that bright, cheery smile, those sparkling eyes. It was all over—I was smitten. Maybe I didn't quite know what hit me at first, or maybe I was afraid to admit that it could actually happen to me. But it was indisputable; I was hooked. I'm so thankful I was.

I remember the first time we talked. I had difficulty concentrating on your words because it was all I could do to resist reaching out and touching your hair, your cheek, your lips. I remember that little twinkle in your eye, that teasing smile—as if you knew that it was only a matter of time. I thank God for that day.

Dear God,

help us never to forget
those first moments
we spent together.
Thank You for causing
our two separate lives
to gently collide and
become so beautifully
one.

Amen.

I Want to Know Your Heart

> Would not God find this out? For He
> knows the secrets of the heart.
>
> PSALM 44:21 NASB

My Dear Wife,

I love what I see inside you. I can't believe how much time has passed since the day we first met. Do you remember those times, my love, when we couldn't wait to be together again, when it seemed we would never get enough of each other? Every word you said completely fascinated me, and I wanted to know everything there was to know about you. I wanted to look right inside you—to see your heart and soul.

I still want to know your heart. And even though we get busy and distracted with our daily responsibilities, I promise you that I will take time to get better acquainted with that little girl who lives deep inside you. I want to understand your longings, your aspirations, your fears . . . I want to know your heart.

Dear God,

You know all there is
to know about our
hearts—things can't
begin to comprehend.

Please help us to
become better
acquainted with our
inner selves.

Show each of us the
other's heart.

Amen.

When You Were a Little Girl

When I was a child, I spoke as a child, I
understood as a child, I thought as a child;
but when I became a man, I put away
childish things.

1 CORINTHIANS 13:11 NKJV

My Dear Wife,

I love the little girl in you. I wish I'd known you as a small child. I bet you were smart and funny. I bet you knew how to climb trees, and I wonder if you had tea parties. Would you have invited me? And I have so many other questions: Did you play with dolls? Did you roller-skate? Did you ever fall down and skin your knee or break a bone? I wish I could go back in time, help you up, and make it all better. We probably would've been good friends, you and I.

Tell me what you were like as a child. What were your grandest dreams and worst fears? What was your happiest time? Did anyone ever hurt you? Were you ever lonely? I want to know all there is to know about you—please, don't hesitate to tell me.

Dear God,

there are so many
things in our lives that
make us who we are
today.

Help us as we get to
know each other in
new ways.

Amen.

Let's Grow Old Together

The righteous will flourish like a palm
tree, . . . they will flourish in the courts of
our God. They will still bear fruit in old
age, they will stay fresh and green.

PSALM 92:12-14 NIV

My Dear Wife,

Y ou grow more beautiful with time. Can you imagine the two of us with gray hair and lots of wrinkles—with steps that move slowly and ears that have grown faint of hearing? It's difficult to imagine, but there is no stopping the clock. You'll look cute when your hair turns white, and my love for you will see past the wrinkled exterior to the you inside.

Let's not fight aging. Instead, let's accept that it happens and rejoice in the number of years we share together. The more I am with you, my darling, the more deeply I fall in love with you. Our love will sweeten and mellow with the passing of time.

Dear God,

thank You for the gift of a companion with whom to grow old.

That is a blessing from You.

Help us to keep our love strong and vibrant as the years go by.

Amen.

I Love Your Face

Ah, you are beautiful, my love; ah, you are beautiful; your eyes are doves. Ah, you are beautiful, my beloved, truly lovely.

SONG OF SOLOMON 1:15-16 NRSV

My Dear Wife,

Your countenance is my blessing. Do you know how much I love to look at your face? I enjoy it most when you don't know I'm looking. I love the curve of your cheek, the shape of your chin, the form of your lips. I love the color of your eyes and the way your lashes flutter softly, like butte flies. I love the way your brow lifts and your mouth puckers slightly when you're considering something.

I love to touch your face, to feel the smoothness of your skin beneath my hands. I love to run my fingers over your closed eyelids, down your neck, over your lips. Oh, darling, how I love your face.

Dear God,

thank You for the little things that bring so much pleasure to our lives—the joy of a familiar expression, the gentle touch of a fingertip.

Remind us to express our love for each other every day.

Amen.

I Need Someone to Talk To

Telling the truth in love, we should grow
up in every way toward Him who is the
Head—Christ.

EPHESIANS 4:15 MLB

My Dear Wife,

I bless you for listening I know that sometimes I might act as if I'm self-sufficient, as if I don't need anyone or anything. But beneath my I-have-everything-under-control exterior dwells a needy little boy with concerns, insecurities, and a need to be heard. Even when I appear quiet and withdrawn, sometimes I just want someone to talk to. If you can gently nudge me out, I'd love to talk to you.

Communication seems to flow more easily for you women than it does for us men. We're not always comfortable saying how we feel—or even knowing how we feel. But you can draw me out. I know you're a good listener; and you usually have something wise and encouraging to say. And I really do need to talk.

Dear God,

help me to become a
better communicator.
And help us to know
when it's time to talk.
Show us ways to share
what's going on inside
us.
Teach us to be good
listeners.

Amen.

Why I Get Frustrated

The Lord will be your confidence.

PROVERBS 3:26

My Dear Wife,

Thank you for your patience. I get frustrated from time to time because I feel the need to be the best, the biggest, the brightest, and I'm not sure why I'm so competitive. Maybe it's the way I was raised or just the result of being a man. Who knows? The bottom line is that everything begins to feel like a competition. If I am taking a test, I want to get the highest grade. If I'm playing a game, I want to be the winner. If I'm running a race, I want to come in first. If I'm applying for a new job, I want to beat all the other candidates.

Anyway, I sometimes have trouble accepting that I can't win at everything and that sometimes I'm not even close. And then at other times, it seems like I can't win at anything. Both cause me to feel frustration. I'm sure you notice, and I appreciate your patience and understanding.

Dear God,

everyone feels
frustrated at times.
Help us to meet those
situations with
patience and
understanding.

Amen.

Trust Me

It is God who is at work in you, enabling
you both to will and to work for his good
pleasure.

PHILIPPIANS 2:13 NRSV

My Dear Wife,

I love how you trust me. One of the toughest issues in marriage has to do with the area of trust. At the same time, I know that trust is critical to a good relationship. I realize that trust doesn't just happen; it is built—one brick at a time—like a foundation. It would mean so much to me to know that you really trust me.

I'm not perfect. I know I've let you down from time to time. But I want you to know that I'm willing to work hard to assure you that your life is completely safe in my hands. I take that seriously, and I pray that God will help me make good on that promise.

Dear God,

please help us to build
a strong foundation of
trust in our marriage.

Only You can make us
into people who are
truly trustworthy.

We come to You now
and ask for Your touch
in our lives.

Amen.

I forgive You

Be kind toward one another,
tenderhearted, forgiving one another, even
as God has in Christ forgiven you.

EPHESIANS 4:32 MLB

My Dear Wife,

Y ou are so easy to forgive. Little irritations—
small offenses, emotional wounds, hurt feelings—build up over time. Sometimes they are
temporarily overlooked, buried, or nearly forgotten—but
not quite. I've been responsible for my share of hurts,
and for that I'm truly sorry. Please forgive me. I also
want to make sure that I've forgiven you. I don't want
to carry around an old offense that breeds bitterness and
eventually pushes us apart.

A vital part of any loving and lasting relationship
must be forgiveness. We cannot survive without it. It's
impossible to love someone without inflicting hurt from
time to time. We're human, and we're imperfect at this
thing called love. So let's continue to choose to forgive.

Dear God,

we choose not to carry offenses against each other.

Remind us when we pass through the irritations of everyday life to freely forgive and to receive forgiveness.

Amen.

We Don't Always Agree

Blessed are the peacemakers, for they will
be called children of God.

MATTHEW 5:9 NRSV

My Dear Wife,

Bless you for speaking your mind. We don't always agree on every issue, but that only means we each have a mind of our own. And that makes life a lot more interesting. We know, too, that sometimes there can be more than one right answer or more than one right way of doing something. Sometimes the best answers come from approaching problems from different angles. One person wisely said, "If we always agreed on everything, then one of us would be unnecessary." And we're both very necessary.

So, dear one, let's agree to disagree. Let's do it in peace. Let's welcome some lively discussions, enjoy a good debate, and practice active listening skills. I know there is much I can learn from you. So I promise to be respectful of your philosophies and ideals. In the same way, I hope you'll respect mine. After all two heads are better than one.

Dear God,

teach each of us to
respect and value the
other's opinion, even
when it differs from
our own.

Amen.

Sometimes I Am Quiet

You know when I sit down and when I rise
up; you discern my thoughts from far
away.

PSALM 139:2 NRSV

My Dear Wife,

Thank you for respecting me. I know how it bothers you when I seem to shut down occasionally and keep my thoughts to myself. I probably look like a grumpy, old ogre; walking around in my moody silence. I'm sure you sometimes misinterpret my quietness and think I'm upset with you about something you've said or done. But usually that's not the case. Usually it's just my introspective way of figuring something out.

Sometimes when I'm trying to solve a problem, I get quiet and stew over it for a while. Maybe it would help to talk, but I don't always know where to begin. When this happens, give me some time and patience. It helps me if I can organize the problem in my mind and clarify its parameters before I discuss it. Eventually I might be able to explain.

Dear God,

sometimes we both
need time to be quiet,
and sometimes we
need someone to prod
us out of our silence.

Give us discernment to
know the difference.

Amen.

I forget to Ask

Rejoice. Change your ways. Encourage each other. Live in harmony and peace. Then the God of love and peace will be with you.

2 CORINTHIANS 13:11 NLT

My Dear Wife,

I love how you remind me. I admit that sometimes I get so caught up in my own world, my own work, and my own responsibilities that I forget to inquire about how you're doing. Please forgive me. It's not that I don't care or even that I don't want to hear. It's just that I get preoccupied and neglect what's really important to me: you.

Help me if you can. I would welcome a gentle reminder that you need to be heard, need to express what's going on with you. And above all else, please know that I really do care.

Dear God,

help us to be patient
with one another
when the distractions
of everyday life cause
us to appear uncaring.

Give each of us the
courage to nudge the
other and deliver a
gentle reminder of our
commitment to each
other.

Amen.

Wanna Go Out Tonight?

David said to Abigail, "Blessed be the Lord,
the God of Israel, who sent you to meet
me today!"

1 SAMUEL 25:32 NRSV

My Dear Wife,

I love being with you. Do you remember when I
used to call and ask you out? Then I'd come by
your place and pick you up for a date? We'd be
all cleaned up and smelling good, and the anticipation
was so thick I could almost cut it with my pocketknife.
Those were good days, and I don't see any reason they
can't keep on happening.

Let's go on an old-fashioned date again. Tell me how
you'd like to do this and where you'd like to go. Then
let's just do it. I'll pull out all the stops: wash the car,
bring you flowers. I don't know about all the details, but
let's talk about it, make a plan, and carry it out—on a
regular basis.

Dear God,

help us to keep our love fresh and new—even if it seems to take a little more work and planning.

Show us ways to make a date special for each other.

Amen.

Sometimes I Need Space

As those who have been chosen of God,
holy and beloved, put on a heart of
compassion, kindness, humility, gentleness
and patience.

COLOSSIANS 3:12 NASB

My Dear Wife,

I appreciate your understanding heart. The work-day occasionally seems to press in from all sides—demands, decisions, deadlines. Somebody is always pushing for something. Sometimes when I get back home, I just want a little peace and quiet—and some space. I need to decompress and transform back into the man I want to be—someone I know you'll want to spend time with.

Be patient, my love, and give me a little space. I'll try to do the same for you, for I know your days can be trying, too, and I'm sure you appreciate this need for space just as much as I do.

Dear God,

teach us to come to
You in quietness and
solitude, allowing You
to refresh and restore
our spirits.

Help us to understand
each other's need for a
little time alone.

Amen.

I Want to Trust You

> One who is trustworthy in spirit keeps a confidence.
>
> PROVERBS 11:13 NRSV

My Dear Wife,

I bless you for your loyalty. I've already talked about trust, but there's another kind of trust that I want for our marriage, sweetheart. I'm talking about the kind of trust that allows us to share our deepest feelings and know that the other will listen in love and never betray that confidence in any way.

I'm talking about the kind of gut-level trust where we can tell each other our worst fears and grandest dreams without the fear of being laughed at or belittled, where we can expose our utter humanness and grandiose ideas and be met with understanding. I want us to trust each other with our whole hearts. It is a comfort to rest in your loyalty.

Dear God,

only You can teach us to trust each other like this—wholeheartedly and completely.

Please make us loving and kind and dependable—and worthy of each other's implicit trust.

Amen.

We Need Fellowship

If we live in the light, as God is in the light,
we can share fellowship with each other.
Then the blood of Jesus, God's Son,
cleanses us from every sin.

1 JOHN 1:7 NCV

My Dear Wife,

I love seeing you relate to others. You know how I love to spend lots of time alone with you, but I realize we need to spend time with others, too. And it can be really great to enjoy good friends together; as a couple. We need to be encouraged and uplifted by others. It's healthy to be around those who believe as we do—people who love God, and are willing to share their hopes and dreams and experiences with us.

So, let's make a plan together, discussing what we both want. And let's agree that we will spend time with others. Then, together; let's enjoy the fellowship God generously provides for us. And perhaps, with the encouragement of others, we can follow God wholeheartedly.

Dear God,

show us when and where we need to spend times in fellowship.

Help us to get in the habit of going and sharing and building relationships with others.

Amen.

Let us do our best to go into that place of
rest, too, being careful not to disobey God
. . . thus failing to get in.

HEBREWS 4:11 TLB

My Dear Wife,

How you refresh my spirits. I look forward to coming home after a long day. Just to see our home—those little touches you've given that make it copier and more comfortable—means so much to me. Most of all, I enjoy seeing your smiling face. It lights up my whole day. Everything else dims in comparison.

I know your days aren't always easy, and sometimes it's hard for you to simply paste on a smile. Let's try to understand each other in these moments and wait a hit before we bring out our expectations. But let's not waste too much time before we embrace and rejoice in our love, our marriage, our home.

Dear God,

thank You for a happy and loving home that we both love coming home to.

Give us patience and understanding as we come to each other at the end of a long day.

Amen.

What Are Our Goals?

> "I know what I am planning for you," says
> the Lord. "I have good plans for you, not
> plans to hurt you. I will give you hope and
> a good future."

JEREMIAH 29:11 NCV

My Dear Wife,

I love making plans with you. Goals are an important part of life and success, and I spend plenty of time pursuing them in my work. But sometimes I forget to pursue goals within our marriage, our family, and our home. Sometimes I get so caught up in other things that I just coast along, figuring our home life will somehow all fall neatly into place. Yet I know I need to lend a more active hand in this area and be a better leader.

I would welcome a chance to sit down with you and talk about our goals. I'd like to hear what you think, what you dream, and where you'd like to be, say, ten years from now. We need to include God in this, so let's also take time to ask Him to lead and direct us.

Dear God,

please show us Your
plan for our lives.
We ask You to direct
us and guide us to
where You would have
us go.

Amen.

I'm Not a "Macho" Man

You bless the godly man, O Lord; you
protect him with your shield of love.

PSALM 5:12 TLB

My Dear Wife,

I bless you for allowing me to be myself. Okay, let
me be the first one to admit it, I'm not really a
"macho" man—and I don't even want to be one.
Not that I don't want to be manly or masculine, but I
can see how the stereotypical macho man just doesn't
make the grade anymore. I desire to use my greater
strength to make life better for us, not to posture vainly
for superficial gratification. I want to be known for characteristics like thoughtfulness, sensitivity, and listening—
qualities that will make me a better person and a better
husband to you.

Unfortunately, I find myself occasionally falling back
into the old macho trap—trying to act tough and callous,
as if I don't care. But I do. That's when I need a gentle
reminder from you about what you admire in a man.

Dear God,

help us both to
practice
thoughtfulness and
sensitivity, giving no
place to useless
stereotypes.

Amen.

When I Clam Up

Anxiety in a man's heart weighs it down,
But a good word makes it glad.

PROVERBS 12:25 NASB

My Dear Wife,

I bless you for your encouragement. Sometimes I do more than simply become quiet. Sometimes I button my lips together and stubbornly clam up because I'm mad about something you've said or done. My clamming up is probably just a way to get your attention. Maybe I'm trying to say, "I'm angry, and it's all your fault."

I know it's not a mature response on my part, and I'm not proud of it. But I'm confessing this to you so that the next time this happens, maybe you can help me. It's these times when I could really use a little tenderness and understanding. I know I don't deserve it, but just the same, it might help to get the doors of communication opened up again. I know our relationship suffers when we're not talking, so it's worth a try.

Dear God,

please forgive us when
we act childishly,
nursing a hurt.
And help us to
recognize right away
that being right is not
as important as
showing love and
understanding.

Amen.

I Need Your Love

Let love be genuine . . . love one another
with mutual affection; outdo one another
in showing honor.

ROMANS 12:9-10 NRSV

My Dear Wife,

Where would I be without you? You are as necessary to me as the air I breathe, the water that sustains me, the food that nourishes me, and God's love that cradles me. Yes, I need air, water, food, God's love—and I need your love; my dearest. I need your love just as surely as God blessed our union. How I thank God for leading me to you! Without you, I would be lost and hurting.

That's how I feel, and I wanted you to know. I realize I don't always show you this vulnerable side of myself, and I'll admit it's a little uncomfortable. No guy likes to appear weak or needy, but I want you to understand how necessary you are to me. You play a vital role in my life. I need your love.

Dear God,

it's a little bit scary
needing someone's love
so desperately.
But then, that's how
You made us, and we
thank You.

Amen.

When We Fight

"In your anger do not sin": Do not let the
sun go down while you are still angry, and
do not give the devil a foothold.
EPHESIANS 4:26-27 NIV

My Dear Wife,

I love it when we make up. I realize that disagreements are just a normal part of any marriage. And it's no secret that you and I don't always agree on everything. But it's my desire that we would never engage in hurtful words or accusations that are spoken in anger. Therefore, I make you these promises:

- I promise never to call you names.
- I promise not to dredge up old offenses.
- I promise to avoid phrases like "you always" and "you never."
- I promise to listen to what you are saying.
- I promise never to resort to physical aggression.
- I promise not to drag out an argument.
- I promise not to go to bed angry.

Dear God,

teach us to live
peaceably together,
but if we need to clear
the air, help us to do it
in a healthy and
wholesome way.

And may our marriage
be stronger for it.

Amen.

I Want to Listen Better

My dear brothers and sisters, always be
willing to listen and slow to speak.

JAMES 1:19 NCV

My Dear Wife,

I bless you for helping me listen. I want to improve
my listening skills. I think I listen, really I do,
but the truth is that I'm often too involved in my
own thoughts to hear all you are saying.

I want to get better at listening, and I know that will
only happen as I practice. It's like shooting hoops—I
won't improve by sitting on the bench. I've got to get up
off that bench and practice, over and over and over again,
until I get it right. And just as I can improve my skills
in any other endeavor, I can improve my listening skills
with you. You make a good coach, sweetie, and I hope
you'll keep on helping me in this area. Feel free to share
your heart with me and tell me what you're thinking—it'll
give me a good opportunity to learn to listen better.

Dear God,

we're so glad You gave us two ears and one mouth.

It helps us to appreciate how important it is for us to listen to each other.

Amen.

Do You Ever Dream?

> May God do what you want most and let
> all go well for you.
>
> PSALM 20:4 CEV

My Dear Wife,

I love when you tell me your dreams. I've shared my dreams with you from time to time—dreams about work, career; our future. But sometimes I forget to ask you about your dreams. Do you have dreams that you've never shared with me? Are you worried that I'll feel threatened or that I'll be concerned that your dreams don't align with mine?

I want you to share your dreams with me—your hopes, your goals, your aspirations. Do you have some secret desire to write a book? To sail across the South Pacific? Is there a landscape artist or a jazz musician lying dormant inside you? Perhaps you'd like to be a small-business entrepreneur? Or maybe you'd like to design a new fashion or create a time-saving system? No matter how large or small, I want to know what's in your heart so I can encourage you to become all you were meant to be.

Dear God,

reveal Your dreams for
our lives.
Give us the courage to
support each other
and wholeheartedly
pursue them.

Amen.

What Are You Thinking?

God wanted the different parts to care the
same for each other. If one part of the
body suffers, all the other parts suffer
with it.

1 CORINTHIANS 1 2:25-26 NCV

My Dear Wife,

I bless you for opening up to me. Sometimes I come home from work, and you seem very quiet about something. You silently go about fixing dinner or whatever, but you keep your thoughts to yourself. Before long, I begin to feel left out. And I wonder what you're thinking—or if something went wrong today. But maybe the lawn needs mowing or I want to read the paper or perhaps I just don't want to barge in on your personal space. I feel torn because I don't want to intrude, but I do want to know what's bothering you.

I've decided that when I encounter those situations, I am going to ask if there is any way I can help. By that, I am asking if you need me to listen. Do you need a warm hug? If you say no, I will understand that you just need some time to think things through and process your thoughts. But it's important to me that you always know I care about you.

Dear God,

help us to be there for
each other without
smothering and
hovering and failing to
respect boundaries.

Amen.

Let's Light a Candle

My beloved said to me, "Rise up, my love,
my fair one, and come away."
SONG OF SOLOMON 2:10 TLB

My Dear Wife,

Your love lights up my life. All right, I sometimes forget to be romantic. But right now, I
want to make a plan to enjoy a peaceful evening
with you, just the two of us. Let's play some romantic
music. And let's light some of those scented candles you
like so much. Because I'll admit it, my love, there is something very special about the warm glow of candlelight.
I love the way it casts a rosy light across your pretty
complexion.

Let's take lots of time to relax and simply enjoy the
soft romantic light and atmosphere. We can talk quietly
and with intimacy, just enjoying each other's presence.
I love watching your eyes, luminescent and warm in the
flickering candlelight.

Dear God,

so often romance gets
lost in the shuffle of
our everyday lives.
Remind us to do the
little things that
rekindle our love for
each other.

Amen.

How Can I Help You?

Each one must do just as he has purposed
in his heart, not grudgingly or under
compulsion, for God loves a cheerful giver.

2 CORINTHIANS 9:7 NASB

My Dear Wife,

Thanks for encouraging me to help. It's not every day that I offer to help around the house; is it? Perhaps I'm afraid if I do, you'll hand me a long "honey-do" list and I'll end up spending a perfectly good Saturday cleaning gutters and fixing screens. Sometimes, though, I want you to give me the opportunity to offer my help before you ask.

I know that's not always easy. But perhaps there are some ways you can help get me on track. Sometimes just a gentle hint will do the trick. A good sense of humor will go a long way. I know you will find ways to draw me in, and I promise to respond with a good attitude. Truth is, it feels good to serve you and meet my family's needs.

Dear God,

help us to be sensitive
to the things we can
do to help each other
and to carry through
on them with a
cheerful and positive
attitude.

Amen.

Healing Our Past

The Lord is close to the brokenhearted,
and he saves those whose spirits have been
crushed.

PSALM 34:18 NCV

My Dear Wife,

I bless you for sharing your heart with me. No one gets married without lugging along a little "extra baggage." Believe me, I'm aware that I, too, have brought along a few pieces of my own. And I know you have some as well. Maybe they are issues we're aware of, or perhaps we have things we'd forgotten or thought we'd left behind. But as we acknowledge them, understanding how old hurts from childhood and youth remain with us, we can begin to deal with them before they impact our relationship.

So, my goal is to share some of those old wounds, the ones that never quite seem to go away. And I hope you can tell me about your own, because only then can we begin to understand one another. And perhaps we might even be able to pray for each other and support each other as we work together towards healing.

Dear God,

show us how to bring
these old hurts to You,
to pray for each other,
and to look for Your
healing touch.

Amen.

Celebrating the Years

Indeed, if a man should live many years, let
him rejoice in them all.

ECCLESIASTES 11:8 NASB

My Dear Wife,

I bless you for the times we've shared. Sometimes the years go by so quickly that we hardly even notice. We become so caught up with all the demands of life and our grown-up responsibilities that we occasionally forget to pause and celebrate some of the milestones along the way. I certainly think that we have some achievements worth celebrating.

Let's remember to honor the time and energy we've invested in our relationship. Let's celebrate the fact that, through it all, we're still together—still in love and committed to our marriage and our lives together. Let's rejoice over our victories from the past, and let's look forward to our challenges in the future.

Dear God,

we've been through so
much together.

Help us to remember
our triumphs and
celebrate our
successes.

And when we
remember the hard
times, help us to focus
on Your goodness.

Amen.

Come into My World

> It is you, a person like me, my companion
> and good friend.
>
> PSALM 55:13 NCV

My Dear Wife,

I love when our lives mesh. I know you think I live in my own little world sometimes, doing stuff like watching ball games, admiring a fine engine, or reading the latest sports magazine. But, hey, my world's not so bad. Once in a while, you should step in and see for yourself. Come on in and check it out.

I'd love to have your company when I visit a hardware store. I'd like it if you could share my enthusiasm for the gadgets that catch my fancy and incite my imagination. And I'd love to have your company when I attend a sporting event. It would double my fun to have you by my side rooting for my favorite team with me. And don't hesitate to invite me along with you occasionally, too. It's a good way for us to know each other better.

Dear God,

show us new ways to
share the different
areas of our lives with
each other.

Amen.

When Disappointment Comes

Confess your trespasses to one another,
and pray for one another that you may be
healed.

JAMES 5:16 NKJV

My Dear Wife,

I'm sorry for letting you down. I know I don't always please you. And disappointment can take its toll on our relationship. Not only that, but I'm sure it affects how much you are able to trust me. And for that I am really sorry. I hope you can believe me, my love, when I say how much I hate to disappoint you. And I really do try to avoid doing so, because when it happens, and it does, I am painfully aware of how it discourages you.

I will try not to make promises I can't keep, and I will work hard to keep my word to you. But I'm only human. I know I will let you down at times. When that happens, please remember that I love you and care about you more than words can say. And I hope you will give me a chance to make things right, if I can, and ask your forgiveness.

Dear God,

teach us to be
honorable in our
promises to each
other.

Show us the
importance of keeping
our word.

Amen.

For this reason a man shall leave his father
and mother and be joined to his wife, and
the two shall become one flesh.

MATTHEW 19:5 NASB

My Dear Wife,

I bless you for valuing me above others. Wouldn't it be great if it was just the two of us, all alone together—living in a little log cabin up in the mountains? Maybe then we might be perfectly happy—well, at least for a while, until I wanted to go golfing or until you needed to go shopping. But in real life, there's no way to avoid all those other people who come in and out of our lives, and it's no secret that they can seriously complicate things from time to time.

I know one thing I can do that should make it easier for you to deal with all those "others." I promise to place our relationship above all the rest. I believe that if you knew how much I love you, that it is more than I love my family, my work, even my best friend, then we could both relax and find peace no matter how many people are around us.

Dear God,

help us to establish
good priorities in our
lives.

Remind us to keep You
in first place, our
marriage in second,
and others after that.

Amen.

How You Can Help Me

God opposes everyone who is proud, but
he is kind to everyone who is humble.

JAMES 4:6 CEV

My Dear Wife,

I love your touch on my life. I don't always act like
I need you—it's just that I like to feel self-sufficient and capable. But, the fact is, there are all
kinds of ways you can help me. And there are all kinds
of times when I need your help. I sometimes give off an
air of complete confidence, but the truth is that I need
to know you back me, no matter what. And when I give
up the bluff and invite you in, I'm always so glad I did.

It helps when I know you support what I do and who
I am. I'm so glad that I have you, honey, and that you add
your capabilities to mine and give us couple power. I like
knowing that I can come home and find you ready to
give whatever it is I seem to be needing. It may be a hug
or a pep talk or a clean dressing for my wounds. And it
helps when you just plain love me—sweet and simple.

Dear God,

thanks for making us
partners for life.
Teach us to avail
ourselves to that
gracious gift you have
given us.

Amen.

There Are Things I Don't Understand

By wisdom a house is built, and through
understanding it is established.

PROVERBS 24:3 NIV

My Dear Wife,

I bless you for explaining I don't like to come across as dense, but sometimes it seems there's just so much I don't understand about you. Sometimes it seems that we just look at things from a different angle, and I need your help when I can't quite see something in the same way as you do. I guess every couple experiences those times when they don't seem to be on the same page.

I promise to be sensitive to your needs, but I know I'll miss it at times. Let me know when that happens. Just tell me: "Hey you, I need a hug . . . I need some space . . . I need a cup of hot tea." Just let me know, okay? I love you and I want you to know that I care.

Dear God,

there will be times
when we just aren't in
sync.
When those times
come, help us to speak
up courageously and
kindly.

Amen.

What Makes You Tick?

I will be glad and rejoice in your love, for
you saw my affliction and knew the
anguish of my soul.

PSALM 31:7 NIV

My Dear Wife,

I love our differences. We have such completely different temperaments. Have you noticed how one thing totally sets me off, but it may not bother you at all? And something may push all your buttons, while I seem not to even noticed Yes, it's a good thing we're 50 different. We can really help balance each other.

But at the same time, I sometimes feel really bad when something, right out of the blue, sets me off. And I can tell you're wondering what's going on. I love you so much. I don't want to be that kind of husband. I want you to feel safe when we're together. Please pray for me that I will learn to walk in self-control on a consistent basis.

Dear God,

teach us both to manage our emotions and to avoid taking our frustrations out on those we love.

Help us to look to You for the spiritual fruit of self-control.

Amen.

I Want to Listen

Love one another with mutual affection;
outdo one another in showing honor.

ROMANS 12:10 NRSV

My Dear Wife,

I really do need your gentle nudges. Without a doubt, I know I can appear to be totally absorbed in my own world. I can get caught up in my career or some project I want to finish around the house or even my own hobbies. And it probably seems like I'm shutting you out. And maybe I am, but I don't mean to. I guess I just feel a sense of responsibility to do my best for you and our family. But just the same, I don't want to be so consumed that I can't pause and take time for you because you're worth it, my love.

So when I'm buried in some project, and I forget that you need to be heard, go ahead and nudge me; remind me that you're waiting—that you need a moment of my time. You are important to me, and I really want to be there for you.

Dear God,

remind us that we're
committed to be
available to one
another.
Nudge us when it's
time to listen to You
and to each other.

Amen.

An Evening with You

Take me away with you—let us hurry!
SONG OF SOLOMON 1:4 NIV

My Dear Wife,

I love it when we're together. Shall we dine at a fancy restaurant, go to the theatre, or enjoy a moonlit cruise across the bay? Or perhaps a romantic evening together doesn't need to break the bank, take days of preparation, or require a tux. Maybe it would be better, not to mention more romantic, to do something simple.

To be honest, all I really want is a quiet evening with you. The two of us all alone—it might even be better if we stay home. Maybe I can help you fix a simple meal. Or maybe we can take a stroll around the block. Or how about a game of chess? But whatever we decide upon, let's do it together—just you and me and romance.

Dear God,

remind us to plan some
special, quiet
moments—intimate
times for just the two
of us.

And help us to
remember that the
important thing is
simply being together.

Amen.

Seize the Day!

This is the day the Lord has made; let us
rejoice and be glad in it.

PSALM 118:24 NIV

My Dear Wife,

I love your spontaneity. I admit I can become too
focused on the minor details of life—things that
aren't terribly significant. And as a result, I sometimes almost forget to enjoy some of the most important
moments of living. Occasionally I need you to remind
me to cease from my activity for long enough to really
seize the day.

I forget that only God knows how many of these
earthly days we'll have to enjoy together. How many
moments will I relish you in my arms or hear your sweet
words of love and affection whispered in my ear? And
when it's all said and done, I won't regret using my time
for such pleasures. I hope you will remind me to enjoy
what we have together—to welcome each new day as a
living gift from God.

Dear God,

only You know the
span of our lives—but
whether they're short
or long, each day is
unique and special and
worthy of celebration.

Teach us to pause and
welcome them.

Amen.

Let's Take a Walk

The leaves are coming out and the grape
vines are in blossom. How delicious they
smell! Arise, my love, my fair one, and
come away.

SONG OF SOLOMON 2:13 TLB

My Dear Wife,

I love aligning my pace to yours. How invigorating and romantic it is to take a walk with the one you love! Maybe it's the warm feeling of your hand in mine. Or the comfortable sense of moving along without rushing. Or perhaps it's the changing season, or the look of the landscape, or simply the rhythmic sound of footsteps falling into pace—almost like a dance.

Will you come walk with me, my loved Can we breathe the fresh air and enjoy some exercise, along with the rejuvenation of our spirits and souls? And let's talk as we go; I want to hear about your day. Or maybe we'll just enjoy the quiet around us—the sounds of birds or the gentle breeze whispering through the treetops.

Dear God,

simple pleasures can be
incredibly romantic.
Remind us that they
are often just a
footstep away.

Amen.

A Five-Minute Exercise

Before the dawn comes and the shadows
flee away, come back to me, my love.

SONG OF SOLOMON 2:17 NLT

My Dear Wife,

I love the touch of your hands. Now I know this might sound a little corny, and I'm usually not one to indulge in such things. But please hear me out. You see, I think we can become so comfortable around each other that we forget to notice certain things—or maybe we start taking each other for granted. So some night, when it's quiet and calm, let's do this little exercise together.

Let's sit on the floor, cross-legged, if we can, and face each other. Then let's reach out and touch our palms together, just lightly. Without speaking, let's just look into each other's faces—I promise not to giggle—and enjoy the sensation of touching palms. Then let's close our eyes and "read" each other's faces with our fingertips.

Dear God,

sometimes, funny little things like this can open wonderful new doors in a relationship, helping us to see each other in fresh new ways.

Give us the courage to try.

Amen.

I will sing of your strength, in the morning
I will sing of your love; for you are my
fortress, my refuge in times of trouble.

PSALM 59:16 NIV

My Dear Wife,

I love knowing you're backing me. Occasionally I want afresh challenge. I want to take on something new or stretch my ordinary world in some different way. At other times, it may seem daunting to step out of my norm and take a chance. And, to be honest, I'm not always as confident as I try to appear. If the risk seems too big, I might not even step up to the plate.

These are the times when I most appreciate your support. To know you're standing behind me, backing me, and cheering me on makes a huge difference. You may have no idea how much your encouragement means to me. Not only that, it makes me feel so connected to you—like we're in this together and our success is shared!

Dear God,

thank You for the encouragement You bring to our lives and the support of our friends and family.

Most of all, thank You for the support of a faithful spouse.

Amen.

Realizing Our Dreams

Help me to do your will, for you are my
God. Lead me in good paths, for your
Spirit is good.

PSALM 143:10 TLB

My Dear Wife,

I bless you for your vision. I have an idea. Let's dream together. We can talk about our hopes and aspirations for the future—whether they seem possible or not. We can discuss where we want to go and how we'd like to get there. Then we can consider ways to make realistic goals and strategies.

But let's not be afraid to dream big. Or even to dream small. And let's not worry if our dreams change—for aren't we constantly changing?

But most of all, let's make sure we ask for God's guidance and direction in our dreams. And let's invite Him to enhance and expand our dreams to match all that He's planned for us—or maybe He will give us completely new dreams. But let's do this thing together.

Dear God,

teach us to dream
Your dreams—and
help us dream them
together.
Then show us ways of
implementing these
dreams—and help us
to realize them within
our lifetime.

Amen.

Just Tell Me You Love Me

My Dear Wife,

I love to hear you say it. Of course, I should know that you love me. And you show me your love by all the little things you do, day after day. And certainly, I've heard those three little words so many times before. But even so, they are so important to me!

Do you know how much I need to hear those three little words? I need you to whisper them in my ear at night. And I need to see your eyes in the morning light as you say them aloud. Somehow this convinces me that you really mean it. Oh, I know it's not only the words, but this is the stuff our relationship is made of. And I won't get tired of hearing you say it. So, go ahead, sweetheart, say it again.

Dear God,

thank You for pouring
Your love into our
hearts so that we
would know the true
meaning of love.

Remind us often that
we need to speak and
hear our words of
love.

Amen.

Let's Make a Plan

The Lord will guide you always; he will
satisfy your needs in a sun-scorched land
and will strengthen your frame. You will
be like a well-watered garden, like a spring
whose waters never fail.

ISAIAH 58:11 NIV

My Dear Wife,

I love how your mind works. How about if we sit down together and make some sort of plan? Maybe it could be for a family vacation or just a weekend together. Or how about a home-improvement project? Whatever we decide, I think it would be fun to do it together. I like hearing your ideas, and it's good for us to cooperate with each other. I know I might try your patience from time to time, but I'd like to learn how to give and take—not to mention how it might help improve my ability to listen to you.

When we finally complete whatever it is that we decide to do, we can enjoy the rewards of our labor. For we'll have learned to work as a team to accomplish something. And, together, we can celebrate our victory!

Dear God,

help us to find a plan
we can carry out
together.

We know it won't all
go smoothly, but it'll
be well worth the
effort.

In the end, we'll be
closer than when we
started.

Amen.

What's Really Important

And he answering said, Thou shalt love the
Lord thy God with all thy heart, and with
all thy soul, and with all thy strength, and
with all thy mind; and thy neighbour as
thyself.

LUKE 10:27 KJV

My Dear Wife,

You matter to me. We both experience daily tugs and pulls on our lives, demanding our time and attention. Often I find the most urgent things pretend to be the most important. And sometimes I mistakenly give those pressing issues my top priority. But if I can just step back and get a better perspective, I sometimes figure out that those urgent things aren't all that vital.

When I take time to consider things, I usually remember what's most important in life. Thankfully, it's pretty simple—almost embarrassingly so. And so, because I love you, my dear, I want to remind you, as well. First of all, I know it's crucial that we love God with our whole hearts. Next, it's essential to love each other. Then everyone and everything else simply comes after that.

Dear God,

help us to keep our
priorities straight and
simple.

Don't allow us to get
caught up in the
tyranny of the urgent.

Amen.

Your Deepest Hurt

For You have delivered my soul from
death, My eyes from tears, And my feet
from falling.

PSALM 116:8 NKJV

My Dear Wife,

I bless you for trusting me with your pain. Perhaps there are things about you, your past life, that you've yet to tell me—or perhaps you've mentioned, but we never really talked about it. And it's possible you may need to tell me again. For it seems certain that we both have some old hurts in our lives—perhaps some we've even inflicted on each other. But how will our deepest hurts ever heal if we leave them hidden and buried? And even if they can't heal overnight, surely we can start the healing process now.

Do you need to tell me about a past hurt, my love? If so, I am here for you. I want to hear all you have to say. And then I hope we can pray about it. Can we ask God to continue the healing work that He's begun in both of us? Together; let's believe that He can make us whole.

Dear God,

help us to be there for each other when it's convenient and when it hurts.
Give us a heart to listen and a heart to pray.

Amen.

Let's Share a Book

To know wisdom and instruction, To discern the sayings of understanding, To receive instruction in wise behavior.

PROVERBS 1:2-3 NASB

My Dear Wife,

Your mini is precious to me. Maybe you enjoy a sweet, romantic story, and I like suspense and action. But do you think (if we really tried) that we might be able to find some common ground in literature? Oh sure, we may both need to compromise a little. But let's try to choose a good book together—one that we'll both want to read and enjoy. Perhaps we'll want a historical novel, or a biography, or even a how-to book. I don't really mind—as long as we both agree. And then let's read and discuss it.

We can take turns reading aloud to each other before bed. Or read the same chapter, separately, and discuss it later. But let's read the whole book, and talk about it, sharing what we liked and what we didn't.

Dear God,

we know it's important to bring our minds together—to experience something new and to grow together.

Help us find a good hook that will challenge and encourage us.

Amen.

Forgive and Try to Forget

When you stand praying, if you hold
anything against anyone, forgive him, so
that your Father in heaven may forgive you
your sins.

MARK 11:25 NIV

My Dear Wife,

I bless you for your forgiving heart. I think the toughest part of forgiving can be trying to blot out the memory of how someone has hurt you. And even though people say, "forgive and forget," it's just not easy. Short of amnesia, I'm not sure that it's even possible. But I hope that as time passes, we can put some memories to rest and move forward.

Each time we forgive each other, let's agree that we'll try to put old things behind us. And let's make it our earnest goal not to dredge up any old hurts from the past, but instead focus our energy on healing and wholeness and love. For it seems that love, above all else, can clean the slate. So, let's follow love's lead—let's forgive, and in time, forget.

Dear God,

we know how vital
forgiveness is to our
marriage.
It's never easy to
forget a past offense.
Please send Your
perfect love to blot
away the hurt.

Amen.

My Dreams

Every day and all night long their counsel
will lead you and save you from harm;
when you wake up in the morning, let their
instructions guide you into the new day.

PROVERBS 6:22 TLB

My Dear Wife,

I bless you for listening to my dreams. I have some dreams tucked safely in my heart—some desires, some longings, some hopes, and aspirations. But sometimes I try to push them down, suppress them, keeping them out of sight and out of mind. It can be unsettling to dream because it often upsets the status quo and rocks the boat.

But then it will occur to me, aren't dreams what life, at least a good and fulfilling life, is made of? And if we quit dreaming, don't we in essence cease to live? So perhaps it's better to welcome our dreams, whether they're big or small, and bring them out into the light of day, discussing them openly. We might even find that our dreams are the same.

Dear God,

You are the One who
gives us our dreams,
implanting them in the
recesses of our hearts.

Show us how to open
our hearts to each
other and follow the
path You have placed
before us.

Amen.

You're My Sweetness

How much better than wine is your love,
And the scent of your perfumes Than all
spices!

SONG OF SOLOMON 4:10 NKJV

My Dear Wife,

I bless you for the pleasures you bring me. Do you know how much I enjoy every little thing about you? The smell of your hair, the softness of your skin, the way you smile at my jokes? Do you know how I love the feel of your hands, the shape of your neck, that fragrance you wear? You are the sweetness in my life, dear one. You are my sugar and spice and everything nice.

And without your sweet touch, my life would be like a cake made without adding sugar. It would be like a garden without any flowers or a rainbow in black and white. For you are my sweetness, my music, my color, and my warmth. You make my world a richer, finer, better place. And I thank God for sharing you with me.

Dear God,

thank You for the
little things that
sweeten and brighten
our lives.

Amen.

I Know What You're Thinking

When my anxious thoughts multiply
within me, Your consolations delight my
soul.

PSALM 94:19 NASB

My Dear Wife,

I love when we share the same thoughts. Sometimes I think I know what you're thinking. And I occasionally sense what you're going to say even before the words touch your lips. Maybe it's because we've been together for a while or just because we're in sync.

And I like knowing what you're thinking. It's not a bad thing, not at all. I think it might be one of the inevitable rewards of loving each other the way we do. It brings me joy to know what's on your mind. So, don't take offense the next time I say, "I knew you were going to say that." Rejoice that our hearts and minds are being interwoven as God planned. Amen.

Dear God,

continue to knit our
lives together—help
our hearts and minds
to unite in
understanding.

Amen.

Around the House

Through knowledge its rooms are filled
with rare and beautiful treasures.

PROVERBS 24:4 NIV

My Dear Wife,

I bless you for your touch in our home. Sometimes I might act like I don't care too much about how our home looks. And maybe I do that because it feels more like your territory and I don't want to invade your space. Or maybe it's just because I'm not sure how to get more involved.

When I look around me; I enjoy the subtle but tangible expression of your personality. But I want to start viewing our home differently. I want to see it as an extension of the two of us—a melding together of our personalities, a place where we can both feel comfortable. I also want our home to be a place we can share with others. And I can see how this shouldn't all fall onto your shoulders. So, tell me how I can help.

Dear God,

teach us to work together in our home. Show us ways we can make our home into a place of peace and order and beauty—a place where people will walk in and sense Your presence.

Amen.

Is Something Bugging You?

Put on the full armor of God so that you
can fight against the devil's evil tricks. Our
fight is not against people on earth but . . .
against the spiritual powers of evil in the
heavenly world.

EPHESIANS 6:11-12 NCV

My Dear Wife,

I bless you for allowing me to help. Sometimes I come home from work and take one look at you and know it's been a bad day. Maybe your lips are tightly pressed together, or your steps flag, or maybe your shoulders slump as if you've almost given up. And, believe me, I really want to help, but at the same time I'm not always sure what you need. So I may just step aside, waiting it out until you're ready for my comfort.

But I always hope you'll soon be ready and that you'll come to me and tell me what's bugging you. Please, show me where and how you've been hurt, and together we can soothe and treat your wounds. I want you to feel whole and prepared to face another day.

Dear God,

teach us to help and to
encourage one another
when we're hurt.

Help us remember how
we need to wear Your
armor wherever we go
so that You can
protect us.

Amen.

Worshipping Together

Oh come, let us worship and bow down;
Let us kneel before the Lord our Maker.
For He is our God, And we are the people
of His pasture, And the sheep of His hand.

PSALM 95:6-7 NKJV

My Dear Wife,

I bless you for your worshipful spirit. Do you know that I need to stand by your side and worship God with you? I need to pray together with you in the congregation or sing hymns next to you in the choir or just silently worship in the pew with you by my side. And when we experience those times, something amazing occurs inside my heart. When we worship together; with honest hearts and open spirits, I feel closer to you than ever!

I want us to take advantage of opportunities to worship together. We need to take time to attend services and gather with those who love God. And we need to remember that one day we will worship God together in His heavenly kingdom!

Dear God,

teach us to come
together before You,
to honor and worship
and praise You.
And unite our hearts
as never before.

Amen.

Over the Years

I will be your God throughout your
lifetime—until your hair is white with age.
I made you, and I will care for you. I will
carry you along and save you.

ISAIAH 46:4 NLT

My Dear Wife,

I bless you for caring for our marriage. Building our marriage reminds me of building a house. If we take the time and invest the energy, it should protect and sustain us throughout the oncoming years. And when I consider the future, I smile as I imagine us growing older together; getting closer; our relationship deepening with time. For I think a love like ours can only improve with age.

Like a sturdy, well-built, older home, with mature landscaping and a handsome patina to the woodwork, I imagine our marriage growing more and more attractive with each passing year. But like an older home, I know we'll have to keep it up with careful maintenance—for neglect can lead to ruin. Our reward will be a warm, cozy haven of love.

Dear God,

teach us to recognize
the everyday increasing
value of our marriage.
Show us how to care
for it as if it were a
priceless investment—
which, in fact, it is.

Amen.

Are You Really from Venus?

God created humankind in his image, in the
image of God he created them; male and
female he created them.

GENESIS 1:27 NRSV

My Dear Wife,

I love your uniqueness. It's no secret that men and women are different, but I believe we are products of God's incredible creativity combined with His fantastic sense of humor. But to tell you the truth, it does occasionally seem like we might've come from two entirely different planets.

I want you to know that I want to appreciate your differences in the same way I would a foreign visitor. I wouldn't expect a guest to conform to our culture and traditions, but instead I would show interest and respect for his ways, trying to learn about his culture from him. In the same way, I want to respect your perspective and opinions even when they differ from my own. I have much to learn from you!

Dear God,

forgive us for the times we've tried to force each other to think the same way.

Sure, we want to be in unity, but not in uniformity.

Teach us the difference.

Amen.

Mixed Memories

It is good and pleasant when God's people
live together in peace!
PSALM 133:1 NCV

My Dear Wife,

I love how you remember things. Do you remember every detail of the first time we met? I think it's printed indelibly in my mind, yet, if we compared notes, I bet we would remember things quite differently. Why is that?

I'm sure it's just because we see things differently—I view life through my eyes and my experience, and you see it through yours. Neither of us are completely right or wrong. We just have a different perspective. Consider two people describing the same house, one from inside and one from the outside. One declares the house is blue and the other says the house is white—and although they can't agree on the color, they're both exactly right.

Dear God,

help us not only to
respect our different
perspectives, but also
to enjoy the varied
interest we both bring
to this marriage.

We thank You once
again for our
uniqueness.

Amen.

Two Hearts Becoming One

For this cause shall a man leave father and
mother, and shall cleave to his wife: and
they twain shall be one flesh.

MATTHEW 19:5 KJV

My Dear Wife,

I bless you for uniting your heart to mine. I remember the day we recited our wedding vows. At that time, I imagined that our hearts had instantly been united by the mere repeating of those important words. But over the passing of time, I've come to appreciate how our marriage union is an ongoing and daily process. No matter how hard we try, that amazing kind of "oneness" just won't happen instantaneously.

Yet I really desire that my heart will become "one" with yours. I believe this happens as we individually surrender our hearts over to God and entrust Him with our marriage. We must allow God's hands to unite us. For what He joins together; no one will be able to separate.

Dear God,

we place our marriage
completely in Your
hands.
As You guide and
direct us, we will trust
You to miraculously
hind our hearts
together in Your love.

Amen.

Holidays Throw Me for a Loop

Forget the former things; do not dwell on
the past. See, I am doing a new thing!

ISAIAH 43:18-19 NIV

My Dear Wife,

I bless you for caring about holidays. There's no escaping that holidays and birthdays and various celebrations come at us like clockwork—and they never seem to stop. But I think I'm coming to realize that due to our unique backgrounds and upbringing, we perceive these special occasions differently. For we both bring a unique set of expectations and customs into our marriage. And I admit that I sometimes forget how we were both raised differently.

These individual expectations can cause us to be disappointed or frustrated because important days don't go just the way we'd hoped. And I admit, it's often my fault. let's discuss these special times in advance and see if we can build new traditions of our own.

Dear God,

show us how to create
new traditions for our
family, borrowing from
the special things we
have each brought into
our marriage.

Amen.

Sometimes I Watch You

How beautiful you are, my darling, How
beautiful you are!

SONG OF SOLOMON 4:1 NASB

My Dear Wife,

How I love to see you. Sometimes, when I know you're not looking I watch you. Perhaps you're interacting with a girlfriend, intently focusing on something in the kitchen, or just rousing from sleep. I like to study your face—the curve of your nose, the shape of your earlobe, the way your hair frames your face.

But even more than that, I like to watch your facial expressions. The way your brow slightly creases with concern when you see someone you love facing a tough situation. I like the way you grow thoughtful when someone asks a provoking question. Or how your lip just barely twitches when you're trying not to laugh.

Dear God,

You have given us so many little things to love and enjoy about each other.

Help us never to take those familiar expressions or unique qualities for granted.

Amen.

When I'm Tired ...

Worry weighs a person down; an
encouraging word cheers a person up.
PROVERBS 12:25 NLT

My Dear Wife,

I love how you refresh me. I wish it weren't so,
but sometimes the everyday stresses take a lot
out of me. And when I come home I'm tired and
fatigued. Like an engine running on empty, I start to
slow down and lag behind. A lot of the time, I don't even
notice how or when it happened.

It's times like these when I really need you. I need
your patience and your understanding and your gentle
encouragement. Perhaps I even need you to remind me
that it's time to slow down, that I need to take it easy. Or
maybe you can point out how I've neglected to get
sufficient rest in my frenzy-paced world. Because the
truth is, I often do focus too much on work and getting
things done—and a loving reminder from you can pre-
vent me from getting weary.

Dear God,

help us both to find
balance in our daily
lives and to remind
each other to include
enough time for rest
and fun.

Amen.

You Are So Beautiful

> Your beauty should come from within
> you—the beauty of a gentle and quiet
> spirit that will never be destroyed and is
> very precious to God.
>
> 1 PETER 3:4 NCV

My Dear Wife,

I bless you for your many layers of beauty. I know I don't tell you nearly enough, and I suppose it could seem that I take it for granted—but you are beautiful to me. And not just on the surface, either. Your beauty begins deep from within your heart and spirit—and from there it flows throughout your entire being—from head to toe.

I know you don't see yourself the way I do. You can be critical of your looks, and you tend to focus on what you perceive as flaws. But take my word, darling, you are beautiful to me. Look at your eyes through my eyes. I don't think I'll ever tire of looking at you. Even as we both age, I know your beauty will remain, emanating from your spirit and flowing throughout your life.

Dear God,

help us to see each
other through the eyes
of love and to
appreciate the beauty
resident in each of us.

Amen.

You Make Me Complete

The Lord God said, "It isn't good for man
to be alone; I will make a companion for
him, a helper suited to his needs."

GENESIS 2:18 TLB

My Dear Wife,

I love how you make me whole. I always thought
of myself as a complete person, fairly self-sufficient and capable. That was before I met you.
Now I feel like something was missing. I believe being
married to you has somehow made me more complete. I
don't even understand, nor can I explain, exactly how
this little miracle works. But I think it's just another one
of God's wonderful mysteries. And I'm immensely thankful for it.

You help me to grow on a daily basis—in ways that
nothing else can. And because of you, I honestly believe
I am becoming a "bigger" and better person. Your kindness and gentleness have taught me to love and forgive.
And I hope there are things you can learn from me.

Dear God,

we are grateful that
You have given us to
each other.

Help us always to
appreciate the balance
and completion we
each bring to the
other's life.

Amen.

The Way We Were

I remember the days of old; I meditate on
all Your doings; I muse on the work of
Your hands.

PSALM 143:5 NASB

My Dear Wife,

I love to remember how far we've come. I enjoy looking at photos from the early years in our relationship. We've sure changed, and I don't just mean our physical appearance. We've changed in deeper ways too. When I pause to remember where we've been, I really begin to appreciate how far we've come together. And I know our love has grown over the years. But I must also ask myself: Have we left anything valuable behind?

Do you recall how we were back then? Maybe we were overly idealistic and perhaps somewhat unrealistic. But did we dream big dreams back then? Have we forgotten some? And how did we see the world in which we live? Were we simplistic? Overwhelmed? Hopeful? I want to remember the way we were—and ask ourselves how and why we've become who we are.

Dear God,

thank You for reminding us that understanding the past can help us better appreciate the present and plan for the future.

Amen.

Let's Turn Down the Lights

You have made my heart beat faster with
a single glance of your eyes.
SONG OF SOLOMON 4:9 NASB

My Dear Wife,

You are the spark that ignites my heart. What is it about turning the lights down low? It's as if something amazing happens. You add a little candlelight, combined with some nice soft music; and it's a formula for romance. I love to see how an intimate feeling settles over a dimly lit room, and how the playful shadows seem to push away the distractions of life.

The world falls away, and it's just you and me, my love, alone at last in our undisturbed and private world. You are my focus, and I hope I am yours. For now, we can sit together, enjoy quiet conversation, sweet nuances, the pleasure of familiarity, the expectation of things to come. So, may I turn down the lights, my love?

Dear God,

thank You for the gift
of intimacy.
As we spend time, just
the two of us, getting
to know each other
better, help us to find
a new level of
commitment to one
another.

Amen.

I'm Here for You

Though one might prevail against another,
two will withstand one. A threefold cord is
not quickly broken.

ECCLESIASTES 4:12 NRSV

My Dear Wife,

I love when you need me. I love the way you always support me, encouraging me in my job, standing behind me through difficulties. And I sometimes feel guilty that I'm not always that supportive of you. But I want to be. And I want to get better at showing it because I do believe in you. I think you're smart and talented and capable.

I want you to know that I'm here for you. I'm standing behind and beside you. And I hope and believe the very best for you and your life. Your success is my success. And by the same token, I will share in your disappointments. So whatever comes, my love, for better or worse, I will stand by you.

Dear God,

teach us to be faithful
to support each other,
following Your
example of
commitment and love.

Amen.

Sometimes I'm Distracted

Accept my teachings and learn from me,
because I am gentle and humble in spirit,
and you will find rest for your lives.

MATTHEW 11:29 NCV

My Dear Wife,

I bless you for knowing when to slow down. You know how I can get so focused on accomplishing something and getting a certain job done that I almost lose sight of what's going on around me. I know how we guys often tend to set our sights too tightly in one area, shoving anything we perceive as distractions aside. But I'm sorry for when I've treated you like that because you are not a distraction. You are the best part of my life.

I invite your help, during those stressful times. Go ahead and gently remind me to slow down and to keep my priorities straight. And if you feel neglected, please let me know, and then let's work together to slow things down.

Dear God,

it's easy to get too
busy and let our
priorities slip.
Remind us to keep our
lives in balance.

Amen.

Please Forgive Me

> Bear with each other and forgive whatever grievances you may have against one another. Forgive as the Lord forgave you.
>
> COLOSSIANS 3:13 NIV

My Dear Wife,

I thank you for your gracious spirit. No one likes to admit it—especially me—but it's true; I actually do blow it from time to time. And I'm sure there have been plenty of times when I didn't say I was sorry—not to mention the times when I never even paused to ask you to forgive me. Oh, I could try to make excuses now, but they would probably just boil down to things like selfishness or pride—so I won't bother.

Instead, I want to say I'm truly sorry for all the times I've hurt you and haven't apologized. And I'm sorry that I didn't always ask you to forgive me. But I thank you for the times you forgave me anyway. Your forgiveness means more to me than I can even say. It's like a stream of fresh-flowing water, quenching a thirsty soul.

Dear God,

You have always impressed on us the importance of forgiveness.

Help us to be quick and unswerving in our commitment to forgive completely, holding no offense.

Amen.

When I Think of You

Build yourselves up in your most holy faith
and pray in the Holy Spirit.

JUDE 20 NIV

My Dear Wife,

Thoughts of you are a comfort to me. When I'm in the midst of a trying situation or I'm wont to understand why the whole world has turned against me, you come to mind. And just the thought of you brings me encouragement and comfort. Maybe it's because I can imagine your loving, tender embrace, your sweet smile, or the comforting words of love and kindness you whisper in my ear.

Somehow just thinking of you brings a sense of stability and peace to my world. And I become so grateful for you, looking forward to when we come back together at the day's end. I look forward to how you'll listen to my battle tales and console me with your good humor!

Dear God,

we thank You for our relationship, for the joy and the comfort it brings to both of us.

Thank You also for our relationship with You, without which none of our other relationships would be possible or profitable.

Amen.

I Need Your Affection

> When I found him whom my soul loves; I
> held on to him and would not let him go.
>
> SONG OF SOLOMON 3:4 NASB

My Dear Wife,

I bless you for reaching out to me. Whether I admit it or not, I have all kinds of needs. And most of those needs are met by you—from a clean pair of matching socks to a freshly pressed pair of slacks to a delicious homemade meal. And then sometimes I simply need you to nestle in my arms, run your fingers through my hair; or tell me everything's going to work out just fine. And it will, with you beside me.

I might not always admit how much I need your affection. Maybe there's something inside us that doesn't like to acknowledge such deeply felt needs. Maybe we're afraid of what would happen if those needs were denied. But the fact is I do need your loving touch—your affection. For your touch reminds me of your love.

Dear God,

teach us to swallow
foolish pride and reach
out to each other for
the things that we
both need.

Amen.

Accepting My Friends

Do not forsake your own friend or your
father's friend.

PROVERBS 27:10 NKJV

My Dear Wife,

I appreciate your kindness to my friends. All right,
I'll admit it—my friends aren't always what you
consider perfect gentlemen. Some of my buddies
are rather rough around the edges, and even I wonder
about them at times! But they've stuck by me in some
hard situations, and they're like brothers to me. By the
same token, I don't always appreciate your friends either.
But just as you and I are different (and we're learning to
accept and appreciate those differences, our friends are
different too.

I know you don't always enjoy being around my
friends, but I appreciate the fact that you are kind and
generous to them for my sake. It makes me feel good to
realize that you try to see good things in them simply
because I do. It means a lot.

Dear God,

You are the best of all friends.

Give us the grace to love and respect the people we each call friends.

Amen.

Your Smile Warms My Heart

A cheerful look brings joy to the heart;
good news makes for good health.

PROVERBS 15:30 NLT

My Dear Wife,

I bless you for your sweet smile. I can remember a time when I bad one of those awful, never-ending kind of days—where no matter how hard I tried, nothing went right. And then, out of the blue, you showed up. Suddenly there you were, just smiling at me. Somehow when I saw your sweet face, your twinkling eyes, I knew everything would be fine. It reminded me that the day would finally end, and I'd go home and hold you in my arms again.

You are the friendly face in every crowd, my love. I count on that smile to bring stability to my life when nothing else seems to work. Maybe it's because you love me and I count on that. Maybe it's because I love you. I just want you to know how much the thought of you helps me through my days.

Dear God,

thank You for the
power of love and the
comfort of a friendly,
smiling face.

Amen.

My Best Friend

There are "friends" who pretend to
befriends, but there is a friend who sticks
closer than a brother.

PROVERBS 18:24 TLB

My Dear Wife,

I thank you for your loyal friendship. I think the best marriages begin with strong friendships. It's like the foundation that steadily holds the whole relationship together. I've watched couples who have learned to appreciate similar things, but more than that they seem to appreciate each other's company. And those seem like the marriages built to travel the distance. That's what I want for us. I want to be your best friend, my love, and I want you to be mine.

I realize it takes time and commitment to become best friends, but I'm sure it's worth it. I want us to depend on each other. So, let's set our friendship above all others. Let's commit to spend both quantity and quality time together. Let's pursue common interests, and let's watch our friendship grow.

Dear God,

help us build a lasting
friendship.

Teach us about
commitment and love.

Show us ways to
develop similar
interests.

Join our hearts as
friends.

Amen.

Let It Go

As God's chosen ones, holy and beloved,
clothe yourselves with compassion,
kindness, humility, meekness, and patience.

COLOSSIANS 3:12 NRSV

My Dear Wife,

I bless you for moving on. Things happen. That's the way life is. Sometimes those things are welcome and sometimes they are difficult and painful. When those hard times come, I've noticed that we respond differently. I just want to deal with the situation and get it out of the way as quickly and painlessly as possible. But for some reason, you seem to want to hold on. You want to try to figure out where it came from and why.

That's when I want you to just let some things go because we can't solve every problem, my love. We can't answer every question. And sometimes the wisest thing is to deal with something and then just move on. But, I'll admit I'm not always 100 percent right about this. Sometimes I need to pause and listen to your thoughts and concerns. And sometimes you just need to let it go.

Dear God,

give us the wisdom to
navigate through this
dance called life.
Teach us how to listen
to each other better.

Amen.

Fanning the Flame

How fair and how pleasant you are, O love,
with your delights!

SONG OF SOLOMON 7:6 NKJV

My Dear Wife,

I love those simple things you do. Occasionally it can feel as if the embers of romance are burning low in me. Maybe I'm tired or I've had a particularly hard week. Sometimes, I'm concerned about finances or a heavy workload. I try not to let the mundane interfere with our relationship, but most of the time I'm not too successful at blotting out the things that press on my mind. That's when you really shine, my love.

You always remember the simple little things that warm my heart—things like a gentle shoulder massage or a certain look, my favorite dessert or a soft, tender caress. And sometimes it's just knowing how much you love me, how important I am to you, how you respect me for who I am, and that you'll stand by me unconditionally, that makes all the difference.

Dear God,

thank You for
providing comfort and
solace through the
blessings of marriage.

Help us to always
remember the
importance of the
simple things.

Amen.

You Are Quite a Woman!

It is hard to find a good wife, because she
is worth more than rubies. Her husband
trusts her completely. With her, he has
everything he needs.

PROVERBS 31:10-11 NCV

My Dear Wife,

I bless you for your many gifts. Have I told you lately how impressed I am by you? Have I mentioned how much I admire all you are or how much I respect all that you do? You're really quite a woman, and I'm thankful God gave you to me. And I know being a woman isn't all that easy these days. I know that it's a juggling act to keep all your responsibilities in order.

I want to learn to be more helpful and supportive with all the things you're trying to accomplish. But I need your help. I need you to tell me how I can lighten your load or brighten your day. I know that although you're quite a woman, you're not a superwoman. And I'm sure relieved— for you know I'm not a superman.

Dear God,

thank You for giving us to each other and initiating the love that flows between us.

Show us ways to help each other more.

Help us to communicate when we're in need.

Amen.

Let's Take Some Time

There is an appointed time for everything. And there is a time for every event under heaven.

ECCLESIASTES 3:1 NASB

My Dear Wife,

I love to be with you. Too many times we say we'll do something special, or we'll go do that when we have the time. But how quickly time can slip away before we actually keep these promises. So, right now, instead of waiting until we have the time—I want us to decide that we will take the time, and then let's not put it off.

So how about if we both sit down with our calendars and make a specific plan together. We can block out some time that belongs only to us—to our relationship, to our marriage. Whether it's a few days away, or a weekly date night, or meeting downtown for lunch—let's get it in writing and commit to do it. We are worth taking the time for.

Dear God,

only You know how
many days we have to
spend together in this
life.

Help us find the time
we need for our
relationship and give us
the tenacity to make it
happen.

Amen.

Totally Devoted

Greater love has no one than this, that one
lay down his life for his friends.

JOHN 15:13 NASB

My Dear Wife,

I am devoted to you. How can anyone ever forget the romantic story of Romeo and Juliet? Those two loved each other so totally that they were willing to die for each other. Sure, they were both teenagers, not to mention fictional—but just the same, I'd like to be that devoted to you!

I know these words are easier said than done, and I'll probably never get the chance to actually lay down my life for you physically, but I know I can do it emotionally—probably on a daily basis. I want to improve at placing you and your needs above my own. I can get better at dying to my own selfishness and pride. I know it won't be easy, but I want to show my devotion to you.

Dear God,

perhaps that sort of selfless, loving devotion can come only from You.

Teach us to love each other so fully that we would gladly lay down our own areas of selfishness for the other.

Amen.

Something You Don't Know

Can you fathom the mysteries of God? Can
you probe the limits of the Almighty?
They are higher than the heavens—what
can you do? They are deeper than the
depths of the grave—what can you know?

JOB 11:7-8 NIV

My Dear Wife,

We have places to explore. Without a doubt, you know me very well—probably better than anyone on earth. But, I wonder if you are aware that there are still some hidden places in my heart—places where you have not yet been, places I long to share with you.

These are things that require time and trust. And they cannot be rushed. But I'm sure that over time, I will one by one open them up to you. And when those times come, we can explore, hand in hand, these hidden parts of my innermost self, together.

Dear God,

so often we hesitate to
reveal ourselves to
each other and to You.

What we forget is that
You know us better
than we know
ourselves.

Amen.

Let's Dance

You will . . . be happy and dance merrily
with timbrels.

JEREMIAH 31:4 TLB

My Dear Wife,

I love how you feel in my arms. How about if we listen to some great music—something we both like a lot—something that makes us want to tap our toes and even get onto our feet and move to the rhythm? It can be fast and energetic; or it can be slow and soulful. But let's just let the music flow right through us, and then let's toss our inhibitions aside and really dance.

I love being close to you as we enjoy the music and the moment and the fun. And our souls seem to meld together as our feet move us across the floor. How long has it been since we've dipped and twirled and glided across our candlelit patio to the sounds of the Beetles or Benny Goodman or Barbra Streisand? So, come on, baby, let's dance.

Dear God,

help us as we look for
ways to relax and have
fun together, whether
it's listening to classical
music together or
doing our own version
of the rumba.

Amen.

Do You Recall?

I consider the days of old, and remember
the years of long ago. I commune with my
heart in the night; I meditate and search
my spirit.

PSALM 77:5 NRSV

My Dear Wife,

I bless you for sweet memories. Maybe it's time to take a trip down memory lane together—to replay our history or just celebrate us and how far we've come over the years. Our amazing story is still being told. And it might be pleasant to hear the words again, turn the pages;, remember the beginning, and maybe even guess what the ending might be.

I want to know; do you really remember the very first moment you saw me? And what did you think? What did you say? What did you want to say? And how about the first time we actually spoke? Do you remember our words? Do you recall our first date, where we went, what we did? And how about that first kiss? What were you thinking then?

Dear God,

we are so grateful for
the life You have given
us together.

We are anxious to
celebrate every golden
moment; for those
moments have brought
us to where we are
today and will guide us
through the years to
come.

Amen.

Total Honesty

*Speaking the truth in love, we will in all
things grow up into him who is the Head,
that is, Christ.*

EPHESIANS 4:15 NIV

My Dear Wife,

I bless you for speaking in love. It hardly needs to
be said that any healthy relationship needs a solid
foundation of honesty and openness beneath it.
And I want us to have that too. So, I hope you'll always
feel you can be totally candid with me, even if it's not
always totally comfortable. Let's not back away from
anything that bothers us. For how will we ever grow and
develop in our relationship if we sidestep the truth? And
isn't it truth that will ultimately free us?

I promise you I will always remember that love must
accompany truth—truth without love can be hurtful and
destructive. And when you need to be honest with me, I
agree to listen even if it hurts a little.

Dear God,

we need honesty in our
relationship. Show us
how to speak the
truth in love.
Teach us to respond
with wisdom and
dignity, and help us to
grow closer together.

Amen.

When Anger Comes

Everyone should be quick to listen, slow to
speak and slow to become angry.

JAMES 1:19 NIV

My Dear Wife,

I bless you for your calming spirit. Everyone gets
angry on occasion. It's a part of life; and sometimes a little loud venting provides a good way
to clear the air and move on. And it can even help us
focus on a real problem that needs some attention. But
I must also admit there are times when anger is destructive. It can hurt and devastate. And we have no need for
that sort of anger.

Anger; like a bubbling pot over too much heat, can
boil over and scald anyone standing too close. But kind
and gently spoken words can quickly cool a hot situation.
A gracious and loving spirit can turn down the flame.
So I ask that you help me in this area, and let's ask God
too; and let's both practice keeping our anger under
control.

Dear God,

uncontrolled anger can harm our marriage. Teach us to control our anger and live in peace.

Amen.

When We Pray Together

All things for which you pray and ask,
believe that you have received them, and
they will be granted you.

MARK 11:24 NASB

My Dear Wife,

I need you as my spiritual partner. I'll admit, it's not always the easiest thing to do. And I can usually think of many excuses why we shouldn't— like it's too late or too early, or we're too busy or too tired. I don't know why, but it usually seems easier to not pray together. Yet it's incredible when we do actually sit down and pray together, because something amazing often happens inside of me. I feel as if our hearts and souls become united somehow—as if by God's power, we become spiritually connected.

But even so, it can be difficult for me to invite you to pray. For some reason I just put it off. Perhaps we need a regular time. Maybe I need a gentle reminder from you. Let's find some ways to ensure that we regularly join our hearts in prayer.

Dear God,

help us come together
to decide how we can
become better prayer
partners.

Amen.

I'm Lost without You

Two are better than one ... If two lie
down together they keep warm, but how
can one be warm alone?

ECCLESIASTES 4:9,11 NASB

My Dear Wife,

You are such a vital part of me. I know you think I'm a fairly independent person—able to move with confidence as I conquer my way through life. And I can act as if I need little if any help from others. But the truth is, if you're away from me, even for just a day or two, I start feeling pretty lost without you. It's a somewhat unsettling feeling. But in some ways, it's a relief too.

It's when I'm missing you that I realize how inter-connected we really are. Like a good wake-up call, I realize how vital you are to me and how empty my life would be without you. For I need you, my love. I want you sleeping right next to me. I need your sweet smile to start my day. I need your hand in mine. For with you, I am found.

Dear God,

thank You for the
comfort and strength
we receive when we
fully understand that
we belong to each
other and to You.

Amen.

How Do I Love Thee?

Her children rise up and call her blessed;
Her husband also, and he praises her:
"Many daughters have done well, But you
excel them all."

PROVERBS 31:28-29 NKJV

My Dear Wife,

I bless you for all that you are. Some people might count their blessings as they go to sleep. But sometimes I think I might like to count how many things I love about you—that's a blessing in itself. For starters, I love the touch of your fingers on my skin and the pretty twinkle in your eye when we share a private joke. I love how you call me up at work sometimes just because you want to hear the sound of my voice.

I love to wrap my arm around your waist. I love the soft feel of your hand in mine as we walk. I love the shape of your lips as they curve into a sweet smile. I love the way you cry at a movie when you think no one's watching. I love you!

Dear God,

we ask You to help
make our love grow
like a well-watered
garden in springtime.
We ask that You'll
show us new ways to
share and
communicate our love
for each other.

Amen.

When We Are Old

White hair is a crown of glory and is seen
most among the godly.

PROVERBS 16:31 TLB

My Dear Wife,

Our love grows better with time. Do you ever imagine the two of us years from now? Will you have snowy white hair? Will I grow bald? With fading eyes and wrinkling skin, will our frames bend with the passing of time? Do you ever wonder if our love can remain as fresh and alive as that day we repeated our wedding vows? I sure hope so. But it mystifies me how something as seemingly fragile as love can survive the effects of time and age—how it can endure the everyday hurts of living.

I sometimes catch my reflection—the aging process in motion—and I wonder, will you still love me when my muscles sag, when my strength is gone? I believe that you will, and I promise that age will not diminish my love for you.

Dear God,

as human beings we often struggle with insecurities.

Remind us often that our love is anchored securely in our hearts.

And as we give ourselves daily to You and to each other, our relationship will grow stronger with age.

Amen.

Distractions Come

I am sending you out as sheep among
wolves. Be as wary as serpents and
harmless as doves.

MATTHEW 10:16 TLB

My Dear Wife,

I bless you for your steadfastness. As I proceed through my average day, I find myself continuously bombarded with all sorts of distractions. Of course, they come in all shapes and forms—a flat tire when I'm running late, a demanding work schedule, an irate boss, an unexpected computer virus. And occasionally distractions come along that would cause me to remove my focus from my marriage.

Who needs to add distractions to our list of problems? Let's both agree to remain careful and watchful and not allow any distraction to drive a wedge between us or cause us to neglect one another. Let's keep our focus on our love and our marriage.

Dear God,

help us to be wise as
we navigate through
life.
Give us discernment
for the distracting
dangers that would
harm our marriage.

Amen.

Simple Things

So continuing daily with one accord . . .
breaking bread from house to house, they
ate their food with gladness and simplicity
of heart.

ACTS 2:46 NKJV

My Dear Wife,

Thanks for all the simple pleasures. I'm sure you know by now that I'm a fairly simple creature. The things that make me happy aren't too difficult to come by. I enjoy things like good food—there's nothing quite like a delicious, home-cooked meal. Another thing I enjoy is the peaceful quiet when we're alone just before we retire for the night. And, darling, Iso value the respect and love you give me.

But too often I catch myself grasping for things that complicate and confuse our lives. I'm so sorry when that happens. Please be patient with me and don't hesitate to remind me that I feel the most happiness and peace when I am appreciating the simple things.

Dear God,

help us each to always
put the other first and
remind us when we
become selfish and
self-centered.

Amen.

God's Touch on Our Lives

God began doing a good work in you, and I
am sure he will continue it until it is
finished.

PHILIPPIANS 1:6 NCV

My Dear Wife,

I love how God is changing us. Something happens on a regular basis as we move through our days, responding to life's challenges, trying to do what's right, working to get ahead—God places His touch on our lives. In those moments, He quietly administers His grace, protection, mercy, and love into our everyday routines. I know it happens a lot. And I wonder how many times I've neglected to even pause and take notice.

I can see God's touch on our marriage, too, my love. Looking back I can see how He's preserved and watched over us, how He binds our hearts together, how He strengthens our love. He even teaches us to forgive each other. I want to take time to acknowledge Him.

Dear God,

we thank You and praise You for Your faithful touch on our lives.

Help us not to take Your touch for granted.

We know that our relationship and marriage are gifts from You.

Amen.

Giving Gifts

You are generous because of your faith.
And I am praying that you will really put
your generosity to work, for in so doing
you will come to an understanding of all
the good things we can do for Christ.

PHILEMON 1:6 NLT

My Dear Wife,

I love your generous heart. It's great to give you
a gift. I love it when I can surprise you with
something special because I really do enjoy the
act of being generous—it seems to strengthen and in-
vigorate my heart. And I know that those of us fortunate
enough to be on the giving end really do get the best
part of the blessing—for I'm sure that it's more fun to
give a gift than to receive one.

But could it be that the act of giving might be even
more fulfilling if we did it together; as a couple? Can we
consider some ways we might give to others—ways to
share from our happiness and from our material wealth?
What a joy for us to live generously!

Dear God,

teach us to live and to give with a generous spirit.

Show us those who are in need and ways we can bless them with the abundance You've so graciously poured out onto us.

Amen.

Quiet Moments

Be still, and know that I am God; I will be
exalted among the nations, I will be exalted
in the earth!

PSALM 46:10 NKJV

My Dear Wife,

I enjoy those peaceful moments. Does your spirit ever crave a haven of calm and peace? I know I sometimes want an undisturbed moment when I can just relax, knowing that God loves me. I think we need those times to experience God's grace all over again. And if we can do this outside in the midst of nature, enjoying God's beautiful creation, it's all the better. I'd love to share some of these quiet moments with you.

So, what do you think? Is this something you long for as well? How about if we spend some quiet time together, doing something we both enjoy, but without the need to fill up all the time and space with words or activities. Instead, let's just enjoy an undisturbed, peaceful interlude—just you and me and God.

Dear God,

show us some special
ways to spend a quiet
time together.
Teach us to come to
You consistently so we
can experience Your
peace and calm and be
refreshed together.

Amen.

We Both Change

And as the Spirit of the Lord works within
us, we become more and more like him and
reflect his glory even more.

2 CORINTHIANS 3:18 NLT

My Dear Wife,

I love what we're becoming Just when we least expect it, change happens. It's inevitable. And as the years steadily move along, we can't help but change ourselves. To remain the same would be to become stagnant, to stop growing, perhaps to even die. And so with life pushing at us from all angles, we must change—we hope it's for the better. But some changes are hard to accept. Sometimes our human nature rebels against change. We want everything to remain constant and the same, but it doesn't.

So let's both try to accept that change really is good. As we watch each other changing with the passing of years, let's applaud our milestones and celebrate these transitions, and let's welcome our new seasons of life with open arms!

Dear God,

You alone are
changeless.

Your love and grace
and kindness remain
constant throughout
the ages.

But we are in continual
transition.

We pray that You will
change us to be more
like You.

Amen.

I Need to Hug You

You have ravished my heart, my lovely one,
my bride; I am overcome by one glance of
your eyes, by a single bead of your
necklace.

SONG OF SOLOMON 4:9 TLB

My Dear Wife,

I bless you for your gentle arms. Do you know how wonderful you feel in my arms? How you seem to fit just right as I hold you close to me? And I love it when you sneak up from behind and wrap your arms around me. There's nothing quite as warm and fulfilling as your embrace.

In other words, I really need to hug you. It's a great way to start a day—or to end it. And, of course, it's welcome any time in between. Your hugs are physical reminders that our love is alive and well. And when I can hold you in my arms, the pressures and demands of the outside world seem to fade away. So, snuggle up in my arms, my love, and remind me once again that you love me—that our love is steadfast and dependable. Let me hold you in a nice, long hug.

Dear God,

thank You for warm hugs and those wonderful expressions of love that You have placed in our lives.

They comfort and sustain us.

Amen.

What I Love about You

He who finds a wife finds a good thing
and obtains favor from the Lord.

PROVERBS 18:22 NASB

My Dear Wife,

I love so many things about you. I don't ever want to get so caught up in the demands of day-to-day living that I ever take you or our love for granted. And thankfully, there are many times, in the midst of my day, when something quietly reminds me to pause for a moment and to remember how important you are to me. How it warms my heart to consider all those little things I love about you. Yet to put these emotions into mere words can sound corny or insincere.

I love the way you put others above yourself. And I love the way your heart wants to do what's right. I love the way you treat little children and animals and old people. I love the look in your eyes when you're sharing something that's important to you. I love so much about you.

Dear God,

we know that You are the source of everything good in our lives.

We honor You now for the great joy and happiness we have found in each other, for we acknowledge that You are the Creator of love.

Amen.

You and I Are One

The two will become one flesh. So they
are no longer two, but one.

MARK 10:8 NIV

My Dear Wife,

I bless you for our unity. I can't always completely comprehend what it means to be "one" with you. Yet I know we're united in our marriage and in our love. But even so, we remain two very different and unique individuals. We maintain our very separate views, our separate personalities; we even have separate gifts and abilities. Yet I believe that God is making us one. It's really quite a wonderful mystery, one that continually astounds me with its dual complexity and simplicity.

While I know and respect that we are "separate" from each other, I am filled with enormous gratitude that our differences don't separate us—instead they make us stronger and truer to one another!

Dear God,

teach us to grow in
respect for our
differences and rejoice
in respect to our
"oneness."

We are amazed by
Your miraculous ability
to take two people as
different as we are and
make us one.

Amen.

When I Strive

Don't store up treasures here on earth,
where they can be eaten by moths and get
rusty ... Store your treasures in heaven.

MATTHEW 6:19-20 NLT

My Dear Wife,

I bless you for your values. Everyone seems to make a big deal about "success" these days. People talk about a "successful life" or "being successful." And I easily fall victim to this kind of thinking. After all, who doesn't want to succeed? Yet sometimes this focus makes me strive in the wrong areas, seeking money and prestige. To be honest, I know that's not how God defines real success.

I need to be reminded how to succeed for God—how to love Him and those around me better. I want to succeed at being a loving husband. I want to enjoy the simple everyday pleasures and appreciate the goodness of a life well lived. For I know that is far better than monetary success. And it's the only kind of success that's gratifying.

Dear God,

help us to know what's really important in life.

Teach us how to keep our focus on Your kind of success—the lasting kind.

Show us ways we can encourage each other toward a better life in You.

Amen.

What I Really Want

An excellent wife is the crown of her
husband.

PROVERBS 12:4 NASB

My Dear Wife,

I love how you understand me. Sometimes I know you want to do something special—something you think will please me. And so maybe you try to do what you think I want you to do. The truth is that my greatest joy is being with you.

I would rather eat a simple meal with you than have you slaving over a fancy gourmet dinner that leaves you exhausted. And I'd rather spend time with you rather than have you rushing around making sure the house is all sparkling clean. Don't misunderstand me, sweetheart. I love everything you do, and it makes me feel good to know that you care so much to go to such lengths to make or do something special for me. Maybe we could even try cooking and cleaning together. That might be more fun than either of us could anticipate.

Dear God,

we have so many daily
responsibilities.

Help us to do what we
need to do and leave
those things that aren't
important, choosing
instead the joy of
being together.

Amen.

True Riches

Flee from these things, you man of God,
and pursue righteousness, godliness, faith,
love, perseverance and gentleness.

1 TIMOTHY 6:11 NASB

My Dear Wife,

I bless you for knowing what's important. Have you noticed how people seem to be more and more consumed with the "big bucks?"—like making a killing on Wall Street, winning the lottery, or being a guest on the latest "millionaire" game show? It's easy to get caught up in all the hype.

I want us to remind each other constantly that true riches do not lie in material things. Let's work hard to keep our eyes on those things that are really treasures, learning to quickly recognize those things that are not. After all, we both know that these earthly riches are temporary, and they can bring more problems than they solve. It's God's treasures that are fulfilling and will last forever. So let's set our sights high, my love. Let's make God's true riches our goal.

Dear God,

help us to keep our
priorities in order
when it comes to
earthly wealth.

Show us how to focus
our eyes and our
energy on You and
seek out Your
imperishable treasures.

Amen.

What Would I Do without You?

Has God forgotten to be gracious, or has
He in anger withdrawn His compassion?

PSALM 77:9 NASB

My Dear Wife,

My life would be empty without you. I try to push such thoughts from my mind, for they bring discomfort and sadness. But occasionally, for just a split second, I have wondered what I would do if you were removed from my life. Where would I be if you were suddenly gone—taken in an instant? The answer feels so dismal that I can hardly stand to consider it.

My faith tells me that God would see me through such sadness. But, oh, how greatly I would miss all the little things you do, the times we enjoy together, and so very much. And because of that, I am more determined than ever to enjoy having you with me right now—to rejoice in each day that we have together—and to love you with everything that I've got.

Dear God,

teach us to number
our days on earth
wisely.

Help us to realize that
any single one could be
the last.

And show us how to
live fully, joyously,
lovingly—and without
remorse.

Amen.

My Comfort Zone

Become complete. Be of good comfort, be
of one mind, live in peace; and the God of
love and peace will be with you.

2 CORINTHIANS 13:11 NKJV

My Dear Wife,

You are my joy to come home to. Oh sure, I know people need to step out of their comfort zones occasionally. And although I usually appreciate that concept, there is one area where I must personally resist. And that's because you are my comfort zone, and no one is going to persuade me to step away from you!

I love being around you! I love taking you into my arms, and I love experiencing your love. I also love taking care of you and protecting you. And I believe that's why God gave you to me, specifically, to be my comfort zone. I hope I am the same for you. I hope when you step into my presence you feel at home, cherished, loved, safe. Let's never leave these comfort zones, my love!

Dear God,

thank You for the
comfort and security
of our marriage.
We know that a good
marriage is a gift from
You.

Amen.

Let's Create a Moment

I am about to do a brand-new thing. See, I
have already begun!

ISAIAH 43:19 NLT

My Dear Wife,

I love making new "firsts" with you. With fond-
ness, I remember the first time we met. I recall
our first date and that first time I took you into
my arms. And, oh, do I remember that first sweet kiss!
And I wonder if we can make another kind of "first time"
moment together. Is it possible to create something new
together again? Or maybe we can do something old in a
brand-new way. However we do it, I want to make a new
memory with you!

Shall we plan a little getaway—an excursion for just
the two of us? Or maybe we could get up really early
and watch the sun rise over the eastern horizon. Let's
dream up something goofy and unexpected. Whatever
it is, we can create something fresh and new—something
we can both enjoy and remember for a long, long time.

Dear God,

help us to break out of
our routine and enjoy
a special moment that
is all new.

Thank You for
inspiring us with Your
mercies that are new
every morning.

Amen.

My Favorite Things

Then he crowns it all with green, lush
pastures in the wilderness; hillsides
blossom with joy. The pastures are filled
with flocks of sheep, and the valleys are
carpeted with grain. All the world shouts
with joy, and sings.

PSALM 65:11-13 TLB

My Dear Wife,

I bless you for sweet simplicity. It's really the simple things that bring me the most joy, my love. Just those everyday pleasures that happen when you live life fully and well. You don't have to cook French cuisine, dress in silk, or get your hair done to push my romantic buttons. Not that those things aren't nice, but my favorite things are a lot easier to come by.

Let's try things like snuggling together in bed for an extra few minutes before we both head off to our busy days, or holding hands in a crowd of strangers. There are so many possibilities, like sharing an intimate conversation for two or walking together beneath a canopy of stars. You see, all my favorite things include you.

Dear God,

as we spend simple moments together, we want to honor Your presence in our lives as well.

Thank You for all the beauty and grandeur in our world and the simple joy of being in love.

Amen.

The Way You Walk

My beloved responded and said to me,
"Arise, my darling, my beautiful one, and
come along. For behold, the winter is past,
the rain is over and gone"

SONG OF SOLOMON 2:10-11 NASB

My Dear Wife,

You have a walk like no other. We can be separated in a crowded mall, and if I'm watching, even from a distance, I can usually spot you. For you have this certain, unmistakable stride that belongs to no one but you. And it's just one of those many unique characteristics that I so love about you. I'm so thankful that God made you just the way He did.

And your sweet smile is no different—it's that light-up-a-room and light-up-my-heart kind of smile. And then there's the way your eyes twinkle when you're happy, or the way you giggle at my jokes or how you hold your head at a certain angle when you're thinking. All these special traits are undeniably you. And how I love each and every one!

Dear God,

thank You for the
unique qualities You
place in each person.
It makes living so
much more interesting
and fun.

Amen.

Whispers in the Night

His speech is most sweet, and he is
altogether desirable. This is my beloved
and this is my friend, O daughters of
Jerusalem.

SONG OF SOLOMON 5:16 NRSV

My Dear Wife,

Your voice is sweeter than honey. Remember that time we had a long conversation, late into the night? We thought we might disturb others, so we tried to keep quiet, talking in hushed, yet intense, tones. But all the same, we weren't willing to give up our little discussion and settle for the mundane world of slumber. We had too much to say and too much to share.

I still long for those private bedroom chats. Those sweet whispers in the night, meant for our ears alone—the intimacy, the sharing, the trust, and the love. And, I'm sure that's what a good marriage is made of. So, let's do it again. Let's talk in quiet tones, telling secrets, suppressing laughter—let's whisper in the dark, my love.

Dear God,

we thank You for the
sweet joy that comes
from sharing this life
with another person.

Amen.

Our favorite Song

We praise you, Lord, for all your glorious
power. With music and singing we
celebrate your mighty acts.

PSALM 21:13 NLT

My Dear Wife,

You are like sweet music to me. Doesn't every couple have a special song? Perhaps it's a favorite tune that was popular when they first courted', something that was performed at their wedding, or just some song that holds some special meaning for both of them. What is ours, my love? Do we have one? Let's remember the songs we used to enjoy together. Let's listen to them again, and let's remember why they meant so much back then. Or consider what they mean to us now.

And if we can't remember a specific song, then let's put our heads together and come up with a brand-new song. And let's make it our own special song—a milestone of the time we've spent together, a reminder of our ongoing romance, a small token of our love.

Dear God,

music is a gift from
You, and it stirs up
deep emotions.
We pray that our lives
would be music to
Your ears.

Amen.

You're My Soul Mate

I am overcome with joy because of your
unfailing love, for you have seen my
troubles, and you care about the anguish
of my soul. You have not handed me over
to my enemy but have set me in a safe
place.

PSALM 31:7-8 NLT

My Dear Wife,

I bless you for your kindred heart. For me to fully appreciate the importance of a soul mate, I need to better understand what our souls consist of And I believe our souls are that inner place where we can appreciate the beauty of nature or enjoy a well-told tale or a really good song. And I thank God for giving each of us a unique soul.

But if we're meant to be soul mates, my love, we need to share some of these same soulful pleasures together. Maybe it's as simple as admiring a lovely sunset, or as complex as understanding an old piece of classical literature. But whatever it is that gives our souls pleasure, let's take time to experience these things together.

Dear God,

all of the earthly pleasures of music, literature, art, and nature are part of Your great creation.

As we experience these great gifts, we thank You for Your awesome goodness to us.

Amen.

When I Blow It

Your heavenly Father will forgive you if you forgive those who sin against you; but if you refuse to forgive them, he will not forgive you.

MATTHEW 6:14-15 TLB

My Dear Wife,

I bless you for your gracious spirit. Just like almost everyone; I wish I were perfect. But we both know I'm not even close. You, more than anyone, have seen, close up, how human I am. Whether it stems from selfishness, pride, or just basic ignorance, the truth is I can blow it big time. And it feels lousy when I do.

But you know what makes the biggest difference in the world? It's the way you react when I behave badly. When you're gracious and kind and forgiving and supportive, I feel like I can pick myself up and go on. I will always appreciate Your forgiving spirit that looks past my faults and failings.

Dear God,

help us both to be
quick to support the
other when we blow it.
Teach us to be
gracious and forgiving.
Show us how to lend a
hand to help the other
one up.

Amen.

Unless the Lord builds the house, They
labor in vain who build it; Unless the Lord
guards the city, The watchman keeps
awake in vain.

PSALM 127:1 NASB

My Dear Wife,

I love what we are becoming. I'm proud of what we are building together—our love, our home, and our family. I know I can get so caught up in the pressures of work or the demands of daily living that I almost forget that you and I are working on something important and big—something significant and something lasting.

I want our marriage, our family, our home to be like a city on a high hill—something that people can see from miles around and that will make them marvel. I want our love to shine like a beacon of hope to those who witness it, reminding them that God is good and grace is real. And I want to build something that will continue even after we are gone.

Dear God,

we need Your help to build this thing. We need Your hands on our lives to make our marriage a monument to You—a symbol of Your love, Your grace, Your mercy, Your forgiveness.

Amen.

Open Hearts

Her husband can trust her, and she will
greatly enrich his life.

PROVERBS 31:11 NLT

My Dear Wife,

I bless you for trusting me with your heart. I know one of the most important things in our marriage is to keep our hearts open to each other. And I must admit this isn't one of my greatest strengths. I suppose it makes me feel vulnerable to leave my heart standing open for anyone. Maybe it's all part of the he-man culture. It's tough for me to let anyone—even you, my love—see what I'm really feeling. And when misunderstandings come, it's easier to just close the door and lock it rather than to let my vulnerabilities be exposed.

But your forgiveness and love can unlock my heart's door. And I know that if we learn to trust each other more completely, we'll both be reassured that it's safe to keep our hearts open.

Dear God,

help us to create a
relationship that's safe
and secure and
trustworthy.
Teach us to keep our
hearts open so that
our love can mature
and grow.

Amen.

I remember what the Lord did; I remember
the miracles you did long ago. I think about
all the things you did and consider your
deeds.

PSALM 77:11-12 NCV

My Dear Wife,

I bless you for all our days. Do you recall that first
time when our eyes met? Tell me I didn't imagine
that unforgettable look that told me "Something's going on here." Or what about that incredible
rush that ran through me? Surely I wasn't the only one
who felt the electricity in the air? And I remember the
first time I wrapped my hand around yours and felt the
warmth of your smooth fingers. You will always be safe
in my arms.

I recall the first time I wiped away your tears, how I
held you close and tried to wrap you up in a blanket of
my love. And I remember the time you did the same for
me. We've been through a lot together—all those experiences, so many memories. Maybe we can take time to
remember them together—and celebrate them again.

Dear God,

thank You for bringing us so far and keeping our love strong and vibrant.

We feel Your blessing on our marriage each day.

Amen.

Planning Romance

> So I decided it was more important to
> enjoy life. The best that people can do
> here on earth is eat, drink, and enjoy life,
> because these joys will help them do the
> hard work God gives them here on earth.

ECCLESIASTES 8:15 NCV

My Dear Wife,

I love that you take time for romance. Remember when we were young and head over heels in love, and it seemed that romance just happened all on its own? It didn't seem like we went to much trouble; being together was enough. Sometimes you were all I could think about as we pursued our times together—times to walk and talk and laugh and share.

But things change, and life's more complicated now than it used to be. And suddenly it makes sense to plan for romance. I see the need to schedule a date or make preparations for some romantic ambiance. And just because these moments don't "just happen" doesn't mean they're any less meaningful. In fact, I think I appreciate them more than ever now.

Dear God,

help us to be diligent
to plan time with You
as well as with each
other—time to talk
and listen and renew
our commitment to
You.

Amen.

Our Sweet Secrets

How sweet is your love, my darling, my
bride. How much better it is than mere
wine. The perfume of your love is more
fragrant than all the richest spices.

SONG OF SOLOMON 4:10 TLB

My Dear Wife,

You are my sweetest secret—and my sweetest
secret keeper! You know me better than any
other person, my love. I am totally at ease
talking with you about anything. What a comfort to
know that I can totally trust you with my most private
thoughts, relying on you to keep them safe and secure. I
love that I can trust you with anything and that you will
never betray me. I must admit that level of trust is one
of my favorite things about married life.

By the same token, I want you to know that your
secrets are safe with me as well. You can be sure of that,
my love. For having someone to confide in is a precious
gift we give to one another.

Dear God,

our deepest secrets are
not hidden from You.

We are completely
known to You.

Knowing that helps us
to confide in one
another.

Amen.

Let's Talk about Eternity

Love never fails. But where there are
prophecies, they will cease; where there
are tongues, they will be stilled; where
there is knowledge, it will pass away.

1 CORINTHIANS 13:8 NIV

My Dear Wife,

Our hearts together, forever—do we really understand what this means? I'm afraid our earthbound minds cannot fully understand the concept of forever and eternity very well. For only God can comprehend these things. And do you ever wonder what it will be like when we are parted by death? What will happen to our love then?

That's when I realize I must simply trust God with such things. I need to remember that He's the One who bound our hearts together; and only He knows what will happen to us in eternity. But I do know this: our love will continue in some shape or form because a love as real as this surely cannot die.

Dear God,

some things are too great for our human, finite minds to understand—things like what will happen to our relationship when there's no such thing as marriage in Heaven.

But we know we can trust You with these questions.

And like little children, we know You know best.

Amen.

Our Love Complete

Christ's love is greater than anyone can
ever know, but I pray that you will be able
to know that love.

EPHESIANS 3:19 NCV

My Dear Wife,

I bless you for allowing God to love through you.
Even if I tried to love you with everything that
I have within me, it wouldn't be a complete and
perfect love. For, after all, I'm only human. Though
sincere, my love often falls short, missing the mark—or
it stops too soon. But I do believe God can complete my
love. He can empower me to go the extra mile and to
love you selflessly and completely.

I want to allow God to love through me like this. I
want to become all that I can be in our marriage—to be
more loving and kind, more generous and caring. But I
know it will take time and commitment, and most of all
God, before my love for you is complete.

Dear God,

You've begun a good work in our marriage.

You've planted Your seeds of love in our hearts.

But we realize that only You can bring our love to a place of completion.

And we know it's a lifelong process.

We pray that You'll help us to cooperate with Your plan.

Amen.

A Shared Vision

Ask me and I will tell you some remarkable
secrets about what is going to happen here.

JEREMIAH 33:3 TLB

My Dear Wife,

I love when our hearts are united in purpose. With time; I know our love will grow and our relationship will deepen. But I also hope we can begin to share a bigger vision for what God might have us do. For perhaps He has united us for a special reason, something that's beyond our own personal fulfillment and delight. And I look forward to serving God, side by side, with you in some unique way.

I want God to bless our relationship that we might touch others. I want our marriage to become an outreach of love and kindness to those around us. For when our cup is so full, how can we hold back the abundance of blessings? How can we keep all God's grace and goodness to ourselves? And as we give and share, we will also be blessed.

Dear God,

we pray You'll give us a clear vision of what You'd like to do in our lives.

Show us ways You can bless others through our relationship.

Pour Yourself through us and onto others.

Amen.

Together forever

Surely goodness and mercy shall follow me
All the days of my life; And I will dwell in
the house of the Lord. Forever.

PSALM 23:6 NKJV

My Dear Wife,

I will love you always. How can we possibly understand the complexities of what our relationship will become when we step into the next life? But as we enter our amazing heavenly home, I want to believe we'll be there together. And how could it be that you, my wife, my closest earthly friend, would not stand next to me with your hand in mine.

I hope I can be by your side as we look up in incredulous wonder at those majestic heavenly gates. And I want to walk with you as we worship the King of all kings. Things will be different in Heaven; I'm sure of that. But I firmly believe our union will remain as strong—yes, even stronger—than it has been on earth.

Dear God,

thank You for this wonderful hand You have created in the earth—this miracle called marriage.

As we continue to walk through this life together, we pray that You would continue to bless our union.

And for that, we give You all the glory.

Amen.

References

If you have enjoyed this book, you will also enjoy
other gift books available online:

Daily Blessings for My Husband
God's Little Devotional Book for Couples
Quiet Moments with God for Couples
If I Really Wanted to Have a Great Marriage, I Would . . .

If this book has impacted your life, we would love to
hear from you.
Please contact us at info@honorbooks.com